T0278578

THE DEVIL IS IN THE DETAILS
The Torchy's Tacos Story

Don Yaeger

ENVISION BOOKS

Library of Congress Cataloging-in-Publication Data available upon request.

This book is available in quantity at special discounts for your group or organization. For further information, contact:

Envision Books

An imprint of Triumph Books LLC

814 North Franklin Street

Chicago, Illinois 60610

(312) 337-0747

www.triumphbooks.com

ISBN: 978-1-62937-997-5

Printed in U.S.A.

Design by Patricia Frey

Contents

Foreword

This is not your everyday restaurant story. What is depicted in these pages is not just the history of a taco restaurant, but an account of the people behind a beloved brand—its quirky culture and its big heart.

Part love story, part biography, part manifesto—this is our promise to not forget what brought us to the dance.

From the beginning, Torchy's has always been unique. We've sought to put honesty and originality at the forefront of everything we create. This book is no different.

The warmth you feel when you walk into a Torchy's restaurant is not a coincidence, but a reflection of the people who built it.

Our very slogan, "damn good food" came from you, our taco fans. So this one's for you.

—Mike Rypka
Torchy's Tacos Founder

Prologue

Fairfax, Virginia, 1991. The sinking sun spread its orange glow across a suburban neighborhood sewer. Most afternoons, teens skateboarded in concrete tunnels and junkies gathered in the shadows but, on this blustery evening in December, even the hardcore druggies were gone—except one.

A skinny 15-year-old boy stood at the water's edge, digging around in the pocket of his blue jeans until he found what he was looking for—a 20-rock of crack. He stared at the white ball in his hand. He'd already smoked through his future, the $25,000 worth of savings bonds for college that he found and cashed were now char and flame inside a homemade pipe. The rock in his hand was the last of his stash and, at the moment, all he had to live for.

A flock of black birds settled on the dead grass beside him, amplifying his solitude, but he didn't mind. He'd grown used to being alone. Crack is not the kind of drug you do at concerts with friends. It wills you to seclusion. It's best taken in silence, and the boy knew this.

He licked his dry lips. In his mouth, the chemical aftertaste of his last high. The look on his face, a sort of collage of love and hunger…and agony. He took a breath—a sliver of reverence, like before a prayer— and chipped a little from the rock. His shaky hands slipped, and the white ball dropped, disappearing into the putrid water.

Oh my God. The boy collapsed to the ground, pawing the murky puddles. He frantically dredged his fingers along the slimy bottom. His broad shoulders, once muscular from high school football, were now frail and heaving with sobs. The sun disappeared, taking the last of the light.

Mike Rypka's cries echoed in the cement tunnel, but no one was there to hear them.

Austin, Texas, 30 Years Later. In the northeast part of Austin, a humble restaurant headquarters sat behind a sliding chain-link fence. In front of the building, a statue of a devil in a baby's diaper perched like a modern-day gargoyle meant to ward off bad vibes. The scowling devil was fixed to a metal globe that read: *Torchy's World Headquarters.* His wide eyes almost seemed to watch as the Range Rovers and Bentleys pulled into the parking lot below.

High-powered executives in fine suits exited their vehicles. They eyed an old food truck in the corner of the parking lot. The big tin box looked like a cross between a beached ship and a prop at a putt-putt golf.

Inside the office, a woman greeted them, smiling, "Welcome to Torchy's Tacos," she said as she led them through the modern building. She stopped along her tour, showing them an array of coffees and teas and a "candy wall" that gets stocked every Tuesday.

The office didn't look like the corporate headquarters they were used to, but it was clean and bright. The people bustling around were mostly 30-somethings, casually dressed and pleasant. The scene smacked of Comic-Con or a San Francisco tech start-up, but with the kind of warmth and heart Texas is known for. Simply put—the place was fun.

The execs took their seats around a boardroom table under an exposed light-bulb marquee that read: DAMN GOOD. A company headquarters populated with tattooed forearms and Vans sneakers was not quite their scene. But profit margins don't lie, and that is why they came.

A middle-aged man entered the room. Formally trained in culinary arts and a corporate chef at multiple Fortune 500 companies before the age of 30, he has played with the big boys. But based on his casual Torchy's shirt, jeans, and sneakers, the guys in the suits weren't sure it was him.

"Mike Rypka," he introduced himself. His smile was as broad as his shoulders as he shook hands and welcomed his guests.

On the whiteboard behind them—the realization of a dream, his dream. In 15 short years, his quirky little underdog of a taco shop had beaten all the odds. Now, before them all, was the plan to open and celebrate the 100th store in an Austin suburb.

"We're just six months out," one of the execs said, going over the numbers. "That will make 100."

Mike listened proudly.

"It's clear that craft-casual has carved a space in the food industry," the exec said, "and you're one of the fastest growing companies within it. Torchy's is a beloved brand. It's fresh, it's authentic. It has maintained a devoted following through seasons of massive change and growth and, most recently, COVID-19."

Mike nodded graciously, scanning the faces of his ever-growing team. In his company, at the very table, were some of the brightest minds in the restaurant industry. They'd left big jobs, corporate titans, and they'd done so to join up with *him*.

After talk of final renderings, another exec spoke up. "There were a thousand places this company could have gone wrong. So what's your secret?"

Mike cleared his throat. "Well, the journey has been interesting. Starting out in a rusty barbecue trailer, just trying to get noticed. And the last few years have been particularly insane…first bringing on market partners, and then, once we had our feet under us, having to endure a global pandemic.

"Last year was tough. Before the pandemic, two-thirds of our customers were dine-in, and overnight we had to shut our doors and adjust to the colossal shift in our market. But…" Mike smiled at the team. "You guys not only did it, you pulled us through even stronger than before.

"This was never about money for me. This came from my soul. Our decisions, our motivations, have stemmed from one desire—to provide opportunities. And when I look up there and see all those pins in that map, all the cities we've reached, it's a testament to damn good people, and how far they will carry you…"

"We picked the Torchy mascot because he was kind of like the devil on your shoulder, encouraging you to enjoy life's guilty pleasures, to stop sweating the small stuff and just eat the fucking queso. We can be playful like that, because a lot of us know what it's like to be on the brink. Thank God, it's not life or death anymore—it's tacos. And as far as I'm concerned, no matter what happens and what hurdles come our way next, we've already succeeded. Where we are right now is far beyond our wildest dreams…"

As the meeting progressed, the plans for Store 100 were laid out.

Mike Rypka smiled. His face, a collage of love, hunger…and happiness.

PART ONE

CHAPTER 1

A Scooter
and an Invitation

If they just tried the food, I could get them to come back.

August 1, 2006. In Texas, in August, you can almost hold the heat. The air—humid and roiling, the sun—relentless, ubiquitous as its deserts.

Just south of downtown Austin, mid-morning light glinted off a trailer. Not the kind of stainless-steel Airstreams that trust-fund babies purchase and stencil with fussy logos, but a dingy, former barbeque trailer, devoid of an engine. A food trailer before food trailers were a thing. A last resort at a time when any vehicle that served food was dubbed: *roach coach.*

Inside the steamy, metal hothouse, Mike prepped his breakfast tacos. Bar towel hooked around his neck, he'd already sweated through his clothes and the morning traffic was just now starting to kick up.

Despite the crude exterior, the inside of the trailer was surprisingly tidy, though splattered with years of grease. Mike had organized it himself, like a one-man captain of a little houseboat. The outside was coated with gray paint—the exact shade of gray Lowe's used on its own buildings. Mike painted it weeks before, on the promise that he could keep his trailer in the parking lot of a Lowe's in North Austin. That is, until one of the owners realized that a dilapidated trailer taking up parking spaces might not be good for business, so he broke the deal. So Mike kept his little kitchen-on-wheels tucked away at Fifth and Baylor, just a few streets over from the bustling capitol building, but the trailer was still too hidden (or maybe too unappetizing) to draw a single customer.

Sweatbands at his wrists, Mike alternated wiping his forehead. With each minute, the temperature rose, literally baking him inside the 188-square-foot enclosure. He looked down at the untouched pile of freshly printed paper menus, **_Torchy's Tacos_**, in bold across the top. It was a simple, get-the-doors-open sort of offering: green chili pork, beef and chicken fajitas, fajita plate, a barbacoa taco, a few breakfast tacos, and a build your own with bacon, sausage, chorizo, potatoes, and green and red sauce. Nothing earth-shattering, but the food was fresh and respectable—and _his_ creation. Mike felt a surge of pride as he stared down at it. This particular morning was a milestone—years in the making—the opening day of _his_ restaurant.

Too bad no one was there to see it.

The trailer's poor location—next to the Tips Iron & Steel building—was Bill's idea. Bill Roberts was a landscape architect and one of the first people to befriend Mike when he moved to Austin a couple of years before. As their friendship grew and Bill got wind of Mike's cooking talents, he suggested (and then nearly insisted) they open a restaurant together. Once the shoddy trailer had been resurrected from Bill's grandfather's backyard, they'd brought it to the downtown Austin lot. Technically they didn't have a lease on the spot, but Bill was renting space from Tips to keep some of his equipment for landscaping, and he assured Mike that it would be a fine place to put the trailer, "just until we get the business off the ground."

But to Mike, the bigger problem was the lack of foot traffic. There were some random construction workers passing by, but otherwise, the trailer was almost hidden. The Ace Mart across the street was convenient though. Mike could just run in and grab restaurant supplies as he needed them, since there was no room for storage in the tiny trailer.

That morning, Mike leaned in the food window, watching the cars inch by, letting the breeze dry his sweaty hairline. The traffic lights stopped the cars in their morning commute downtown and created a backup for a couple of blocks.

If they just tried the food, I could get them to come back.

"Yo, Mike!" The call broke Mike from his daydream. He looked out across the parking lot as Bill's truck pulled up. "How's the first day?"

"Well, you're the first person I've seen," Mike said dryly. "Except for Juan."

Bill nodded at Juan who stood sweating over the grill. Juan had been a line cook at Lucy's Boatyard but left to become Torchy's first and only employee.

"In that case, make me an egg taco," Bill said as he climbed down from the cab.

"Seen your landlord this morning?" Mike asked, slightly anxious.

"No, but stop worrying about it. We talked about it. He knows we're here."

"Hard not to worry when all you've got is a food permit and a handshake." Mike slapped some margarine on the flat top grill, thinking as it hissed. He assembled the perfect egg taco and handed it through the order window. "Bill, I'm dying here. Not only are we doing tacos in Texas, we're hiding them in this tin can. There's gotta be a better way of getting people's attention."

"*We will.* Give it time…I was actually thinking we take some cash from whatever we make this week and print up some Torchy's T-shirts."

"Shirts?" Mike snorted. "How about we start with tortillas? We owe El Milagro 100 bucks already. You're putting the cart before the horse again."

"It's all about advertising, Mikey," Bill said.

"You're in lawn care." Mike's tone was jovial, but he was serious.

A few more seconds passed with only the hissing of the grill between them. Then, Mike had an idea.

"Stay here for a few minutes and watch the window." Mike took off his apron and began loading Styrofoam to-go ramekins with fresh salsa into a cooler.

Bill shot his partner a confused look. "I've got to deliver some boxwoods across town in an hour."

"If the people won't come to the tacos, I'll take the tacos to them. We're gonna need chips—lots of chips!"

Mike grabbed a handful of the paper menus and jumped from the top stair of the trailer, landing with a thud. He stumbled excitedly to his red Vespa, securing the cooler of salsa and chips to the back of it. "Be back in a few minutes…it's time to preach!"

Mike flipped down the visor of his helmet as he mounted the red scooter and zipped out into the morning traffic.

Fast forward a couple of weeks, and Mike's plan of taking the food to the people had actually started to work. The chips and salsa were not only appreciated, they were devoured, and suddenly, Mike's phone started to ring. To-go orders. Deliveries. Even a few catering requests. The interest was so great that he went back to Lucy's Boatyard (the restaurant where he used to work) to solicit help from his old server friends.

The plan was simple. The servers would be his missionaries of sorts, but instead of handing out religious tracts, they'd give out menus and delicious tacos.

"All I'm asking is that you show up," Mike told the servers. "You smile…give people sitting in their cars a free breakfast taco…and then tell them to call us."

On one of those days, while soliciting help at Lucy's, Mike ran into his old buddy Jay Wald. Mike and Jay had worked together at Lucy's Boatyard. Though Jay was a little younger than Mike, both men were lifers in the restaurant industry. They were also entrepreneurs at heart who had the ability to work under someone but secretly dreamed of doing their own thing. They'd even talked of doing it together.

"It's all happening, Jay," Mike said to him. "I know you're tired of the corporate grind. You could join me."

Jay laughed. "You know I love you, but you're slinging tacos from the back of your scooter. I can't go to my wife and tell her I'm quitting a steady job for that."

"We're getting some real traction," Mike coaxed.

"Just keep at it." Jay gave him a hug.

"I'm gonna ask again," Mike said. "It's gonna work, you'll see."

But for the young servers at Lucy's Boatyard, it didn't take much convincing to get them to temporarily join Mike's ranks. Free coffee and all the breakfast tacos they could eat before their shifts at Lucy's was a pretty sweet deal. They could also pocket any tips from the lucky taco recipients.

Every morning, Mike loaded their coolers, handed them a stack of menus, and sent them on foot into the morning traffic. This was the beginning of the word-of-mouth advertising that would be the wind in Mike's sail for years to come. The gospel was spreading, so much so that some people were even beginning to look up the address on the menu so they could pay him an in-person visit.

The slow snowball of calls and the occasional regulars on foot made for a baseline clientele, but money remained tight. Some mornings Mike would only have enough cash to buy one sleeve of paper boats, so after he'd made a little money from the breakfast rush, he'd get Juan to watch the grill while he ran across the street to the Ace Mart for another sleeve.

Those days were hand to mouth, but with a lot of heart. Bill would come and go but Mike and Juan were easily putting in 100-hour weeks, and that was enough to keep their spirits buoyed up and the tin can of tacos afloat. Until the afternoon they finally heard from the landlord of Tips.

Bill had bumped into him one afternoon after the trailer had been running for a couple of weeks. He told the landlord that the taco business was off the ground, and they wanted to give him a little bit of money for the space. A few days later, the landlord slapped Bill with an invoice.

"Twenty-five hundred bucks? We're not paying that," Bill told Mike. "Don't worry, I'll talk him down."

But a few more days passed, and the invoice went unpaid. The landlord, having clearly run out of patience, marched over to the trailer in the middle of the lunch rush and took an ax to the powerline, killing the electricity by literally cutting the cord in half.

Mike stood cursing with Juan in the darkened trailer. He stepped out and apologized to the guests who were waiting for lunch. "Technical difficulties," he said, trying not to seem panicked. "Gonna need to shut her down for the day, but we'll be back up soon. So sorry about that."

Together, Mike and Juan stood in back of the trailer and stared at the thick severed power cord, wires exposed.

Juan sighed and clicked his teeth. "What do we do now, boss?"

Mike pulled out his cellphone. "We call Bill."

Like a cat, Bill always seemed to land on his feet. Instead of getting down about their abrupt eviction from Fifth and Baylor, he suggested that Mike move the Torchy's trailer to the driveway of his home until they figured things out.

"It's not ideal, but it's only two miles away. You'll still be downtown," Bill said.

Since there was no alternative, Mike stayed the course. He set up at Bill's house, sweating in the late August heat with Juan at his side. They still had their food permit, but Mike knew that cooking in this capacity, in Bill's front yard, was definitely breaking some major health codes. It was also hot. Very hot. With temperatures soaring above 100 degrees outside and the heat from the grill inside, the tiny AC unit didn't even put a dent in the heat. The wall of the metal can was so hot, it burned Mike's back when he accidentally brushed against it.

"You want me to make more potatoes?" Juan asked on their second morning in the driveway.

"Of course." Mike wiped the order window with a rag. "It's almost 9 o'clock."

"But no one is here," Juan said softly.

Mike kept his head down. He didn't need to peer out across the quiet street to confirm that they were completely alone.

Again, there was just the sound of the grill.

"You're right. I make double this time," Juan said, trying to be optimistic. He slapped some grease onto the flattop, and suddenly, Mike's phone buzzed.

"Hello," Mike said. "…yeah, we've had a few issues. We're actually in the process of relocating, but tell me what you need," he said excitedly into the receiver. "For 15 people? Give us 30 minutes."

Mike hung up and smiled at Juan. "You seen the movie *Field of Dreams*?"

Juan shook his head no.

"Well, I'll spoil it for you—build it, and they will freaking come."

CHAPTER 2

The World Bank

Young and intimidated, so what? I'll show them what working hard looks like.

Fairfax, Virginia, 1998. A decade and a half before there was an old trailer glinting in the Austin heat, there was a 22-year-old kid moving back in with his mother.

Fresh out of a rigorous culinary arts program at Johnson and Wales University in Miami, young Mike was ready to work. He'd already held positions in a number of kitchens in South Florida, but now he was ready to take some bigger steps, maybe even find a role as head chef.

Of course, he also dreamed of starting his own restaurant. A daunting task for anyone, particularly a 20-something kid with no money. Still, it was the beginning of a dream. But Mike knew its execution would have to wait.

He was pretty proud of what he'd accomplished already. Despite bumps in his early academic career, he finished culinary school. So naturally it made sense to come back home and blow off a little steam. He'd worked hard (and done so while keeping his nose clean), so he was entitled to a little break. He picked up a few shifts in the kitchen at the country club where he'd worked as a teen, but for the most part, he was unemployed, just beginning to mentally sketch some of the restaurant concepts that would one day be Torchy's.

But as it sometimes goes for young dreamers, the meager money he'd saved disappeared pretty quickly. A couple months passed, and before he knew it, he'd charged up a few credit cards. He was starting to feel that the break time was over, and then looking over at his tired single mom as she came in from work one evening—exhaustion all over her face—he knew: *it's time to buckle down and get a job.*

Mike began searching and asking around, but even with his solid resume, he wasn't really sure where to start until his mom's boyfriend made a suggestion one evening.

"I saw there's some sort of culinary position needed at the Marriott in downtown D.C. Send me your resume, and I'll see if I can get you an interview."

"Sounds good," Mike obliged, not thinking much of it. At the time, he had his sights set on Sysco, a broadline food distributor. Maybe as a sales rep. It wasn't his dream job, but he liked the thought of going from store to store. He figured he was personable enough for sales, and it would keep him in the food industry.

But then, just a few days later, Mike got a call.

"Mr. Rypka, I'm with Marriott. We've looked at your resume, and we'd like you to come and interview with us at the World Bank in D.C."

"Absolutely. Sure thing," Mike said excitedly.

He hung up the phone. *The World Bank? What the hell is that?*

After a couple of interviews with Marriott's corporate dining side, Mike was offered the job. "I'm going to be the assistant manager at the World Bank in D.C.," he told his mother excitedly.

The salary? A whopping $28,000 a year. To a broke kid in the 1990s, the starting pay wasn't chump change, but Mike definitely wasn't doing it for the money. Once Mike figured out what exactly the World Bank was, he was intrigued. There was literally no limit to what he could learn. The role felt grown up. Mature. (And not just because he'd have to show up in a suit and tie every day.) Just the sheer scope of the high-profile account was enticing. The café was essentially a giant food bazaar, exclusively serving the employees of the World Bank and their invited guests—3,000 to 4,000 people daily—for breakfast and lunch. The global food court had 13 stations, each representing a different region of the world: Mediterranean, Asian, French, South African, Indian…and so on. They also had a salad bar, grill, dessert counter, sushi station, and deli.

This would not be the last time that Mike would find himself on the cusp of a trend years before it was commonplace. Though "food halls" started gaining traction in the early 2000s, serving fresh food from all over the world—in one single location—was an exotic and unusual concept in 1998. This wasn't the typical pizza and Chinese food offered at the Springfield Mall where Mike went as a kid.

At the World Bank, the menu called for 52 entrées a day, not counting what was offered on the grill and in the deli and at the sushi station. The menu changed every day for six weeks, and then the cycle repeated itself. Early on, Mike went from station to station, trying to get the lay of the land before he even began to think about committing hundreds and hundreds of recipes to memory. Thankfully, there were a few consistencies, "Prime Rib Wednesdays," for instance.

To further complicate things, all the items at the café were made from scratch—no shortcuts. No frozen beef patties on a chafing dish. It was labor intensive—homemade sauces, hand-rolled spring rolls. On his first day "at the office," just the sheer volume of the food coming into the kitchen was overwhelming for Mike. He joined in unloading the white rice—pallets and pallets of it. It was astounding. He'd experienced all kinds of cuisine in Miami but watching the delivery trucks took his global education to the next level. One of his first lessons: people across the world eat *a lot* of rice.

A month and a half into his new role, Mike was starting to get into a groove when a bomb got dropped: his boss was leaving to take a general manager position elsewhere. And who did they want as his replacement? Mike.

As much as Mike felt the culinary training had prepared him for the role, he was also shocked. He was just barely into the new gig, and there was still so much to learn about the new company. He didn't feel ready, but the challenge was too enticing. He had to take the job.

How hard can it be? he thought.

For the new responsibilities—leading a kitchen crew of 75 people—Mike got a raise: four grand, putting him at a whopping $32,000 a year plus benefits. He knew the salary was low, but again, it wasn't about the cash so much as the potential—the opportunity.

But the enthusiasm Mike had as head chef was short-lived. The kitchen staff (most of whom were at least a decade older than him) mocked the fresh-faced kid. He quickly realized that when they called him "boss," it was not out of respect but contempt. In addition to the 75 people in the kitchen, there were 14 dishwashers, so he was outnumbered almost 100 to one.

He didn't really know what to do, until he sought guidance from a new friend, Kim San, a chef at a different Marriott unit who dealt with executive dining. Kim had actually started the World Bank Cafe in the first place, so when he pulled Mike aside, Mike was all ears.

"Listen," Kim told him. "Just because you're a little inexperienced doesn't mean you don't deserve to be here. How old are you anyway?"

"Twenty-two," Mike said under his breath.

"OK, so you're young. So what? Work harder than anyone else. But not just that—*let them see you work.* Get down on their level. A lot of chefs come in here, and they don't like to work. The guys might naturally think you're lazy because you're white, and you got a job, and it's easy for you. Prove them wrong. Show them you can work."

Mike heeded the advice. Not only did he join in the grunt work himself, he tried to make things a game. He put on little contests in which he, too, would participate.

"Let's see who can be the first to break down this case of broccoli!" he'd challenge the crew.

Each day Mike told himself one thing: *Make sure you're the hardest working person in the room.*

With some of the older ladies in the kitchen, Mike took a different approach. He employed his best Southern gentleman, opening doors and carrying heavy dishpans. "Let me get that for you," he'd say.

And with everyone on staff, he used these phrases again and again: "What are you doing? What do you need? How can I help you?"

His original goal was earning the respect of his crew, but in the process, Mike found himself making real relationships. He asked about their lives and families. His genuine interest in his staff resulted in respect…even friendships. For the first time in his adult life, he was captain of his own team.

This foundation would prove important, because a few months later, Mike would be approached with another request.

"We've had the same menu for about three years," Mike's bosses told him one morning. "We think it's getting a little stale. What would you say to freshening it up?"

"Freshening it up?" Mike asked. "As in…?"

"Well, in a perfect world, we'd have you redo the whole thing. But we'll settle for a good facelift."

Mike swallowed hard. If he'd been honest, he hadn't had time to learn the first menu completely yet. For instance, the guys who'd been preparing the Hunan chicken, well, he'd just trusted them to make it their way. He'd been so busy trying to assist everybody and win their approval from a managerial standpoint there hadn't been enough time in the day for him to also commit all the recipes to memory.

But again, Mike accepted the challenge without showing his hand. "I'll give it a try," he said.

Redo the World Bank menu?

The notion was almost as absurd as rewriting the Bible. Before him, a literal world of recipes to choose from. When he thought about it that way, he could feel himself drifting into decision fatigue. The menu was so expansive, he didn't really know where to begin, but he was getting used to teetering on the edge of excited and overwhelmed. He dug deep. More than pleasing his bosses with fancy new recipes, his first goal was to satisfy his global clientele. To give them a taste of their home country. And personally, he wanted to see just how creative he could be.

But there was also the business side of things to consider. The food at the World Bank was heavily subsidized. An eight-ounce prime rib was only five bucks. At the time Mike started, the café posted about $16,000 in sales on its very best day, and the average plate was three or four bucks. Mike didn't have to be good at math to know that meant a crap-ton of customers to get those kinds of numbers. It was a tricky game, but it presented Mike with his earliest lessons on profit and loss.

He talked about it with his mother that evening.

"How are you feeding 4,000 people a day on $16,000 tops?" she asked. "That's like the miracle of the loaves and fishes."

"Very carefully," Mike said.

As far as he was concerned, making money would simply mean not losing it.

Mike began the daunting task of revamping about 600 recipes. Since he couldn't afford to buy research materials on his modest income, he did what any knowledge-hungry kid did before the age of the internet: he went to Barnes & Noble. He bought a coffee and sat at a table in the corner, thumbing through stacks of cookbooks, taking furious notes.

Mike also studied the current World Bank recipes. "Let's see what's in the pad thai," he said, thumbing through the massive recipe binder. "Brown sugar? They don't have freakin brown sugar in Thailand. That's gotta go."

If his ultimate goal was making world-class recipes, Mike realized he'd have to get as close as possible to the original source. Bookstores provided a nice pool of ideas, but he had to get even closer.

With a crew of 100, in a city like D.C., there was no shortage of ethnic diversity. By his count, there were 22 different countries represented in his large staff.

"Tell me about your favorite traditional dish," Mike said to the cultural melting pot of coworkers in his kitchen.

It didn't matter who he was talking to, the answer was always some variation of the same thing.

"I don't really know the recipe, but my grandmother does."

Mike heard that phrase again and again, and it hit him—*this is the secret ingredient*. He had to get the recipes from the people who were still making these traditional dishes in the traditional way. He needed the mothers and grandmothers.

So, he gave the crew some homework: "Go visit Grandma and get me those recipes."

And to his surprise, many of them actually accepted the challenge and returned with soiled scraps of handwritten recipes. Most of the time, the notes were not exactly self-explanatory. So, as much as he could, Mike would ask those who brought in the recipes to test them out with him. "Sit down and let's try this thing out together," he'd say.

This empowered them. They were contributing to the legacy. The low men on the totem pole were suddenly sitting with the chef, making Cousin So-and-So's tamales which would soon be shared with thousands of people.

But in some instances, the recipe retrieval turned up nothing, so Mike had to take yet another step. This was particularly true when it came to the mole (a spiced Mexican sauce made from chocolate and chilis and usually served with meat).

One of Mike's favorite dishwashers, Ramon, had been bragging to Mike that his grandmother's mole recipe was "the best in the world." But there was one problem—she couldn't really speak English, much less write it down for him.

"Well, there's only one thing to do," Mike said. "Let's go see her."

"You want to go with me? To my grandmother's house?" he asked.

"If you say her mole recipe can't be beat, then I need to know how she does it."

"She lives in Arlington."

"We'll go on my off day," Mike said. "How about Sunday?"

"She has church in the morning, but we can go in the afternoon. Sundays she cooks for my whole family anyway, so you can watch her make the mole."

"Perfect. I'll pick you up."

A few days later, Mike was sitting in the kitchen of a little elderly woman from Oaxaca, feeling the kind of rush he hadn't felt since he served global leaders on Fisher Island. It was the opposite end of the spectrum from the posh island community but being in the humble kitchen of an 80-year-old Mexican woman, Mike's excitement level was the same.

"Thank you for having me," Mike bowed politely to the grandmother as Ramon introduced him.

The woman smiled, revealing a few missing teeth. She spoke rapidly in Spanish.

"She says she's honored to give her recipe to the place where her grandson works," Ramon interpreted.

She motioned Mike closer and he watched as she dropped the chilies into the oil.

"What's she saying?" Mike asked Ramon.

"She says do the chilies first, then the seeds."

Mike nodded, scribbling in his notebook, noting the muscle memory of the woman's cooking—no measuring cups or spoons. The quantities of spices eyeballed after decades of practice.

Once she gave the okay, Mike dipped a wooden spoon into the spicy brown sauce.

She watched his face, trying to read his response.

"Pretty goddamn amazing," Mike said with a laugh. He turned to the grandmother. "I hope I can do this recipe justice…thank you for sharing it with me."

FOR MIKE, ONE BIG takeaway from the World Bank experience was the universality of certain ingredients. Sure, at Johnson and Wales, every day was an interplay of innovation and fundamentals, but here, different cultures were right in front of him, putting different twists on the very same thing.

The habanero was the perfect example of this. People in the Caribbean use habaneros a certain way. People in Africa use them a certain way. People in Central America use them a certain way. Working with and for such a diverse clientele, Mike was exposed to all three ways of using the pepper. The versatility of certain ingredients was something that would stay with him for years down the road in his ongoing pursuit of unique flavor palates.

Only a couple of months into his task, Mike had redone close to 60 percent of the menu. And of the remaining 40 percent, he revamped much of that. Sometimes just a few small tweaks made a world of difference. "This one needs a little more salt," he'd conclude. "This sauce is too thin."

Once the menu revision was complete, it wasn't long before his efforts were reflected in the bottom line. The average sales for the World Bank started going up. If $16,000 was the record high when Mike started, that sales number soon became the average. In a short time, the daily sales high topped $23,000.

This kind of boost was just what Mike needed. It gave him the confidence to look for other ways to generate influence and create attention for the café. Among them was an accidental ambassadorship. No, he wasn't writing policy, but on Prime Rib Wednesdays, Mike made the executive decision to bring in Argentinian beef. Patrons loved it. The Argentinians working at the World Bank loved it. So much so that Mike was invited as a special guest to the Embassy of Argentina.

As satisfied as he was with his role, Mike knew there was more out there, particularly from an economic standpoint. The workload at the World Bank might have been never-ending, but the pay was not. Mike felt a little embarrassed if anybody ever found out how little he was actually bringing in. He knew he was young and lacked head chef experience, but he also happened to know that the chef that preceded him made $60,000 a year. And he was at just over half of that.

So, during a vacation to Los Angeles, Mike casually sent around his resume within the Marriott ranks. Just to see if anyone would bite.

And immediately, they did.

MTV in Santa Monica (also a Marriott account) had a job opening in their culinary department, so they called Mike up. "We were hoping for an in-person interview while you're still in town," they said.

Once again, somewhat to his own surprise, Mike was a hit. The salary was still modest, but much closer to a number he could live with, so before leaving California, he accepted the role of executive chef and went back to D.C., knowing this was the end of his season at the World Bank.

Mike turned in his notice and worked out the next few weeks. On his last day, the very same people who mocked and made fun of him, calling him "kid," were gathered around him, crying. A few of them even begged him to stay.

The whole kitchen lined up and sang "For He's a Jolly Good Fellow." Never in the history of the World Bank had someone had that kind of sendoff. They'd pooled their money and bought Mike a gift: a beautiful box of cigars with a fancy ashtray, cutter, and a lighter.

"We love you," they said. "Sometimes when you're just working in the kitchen, you feel stuck and unimportant. But you saw value in us. You're one of the best bosses we've ever had."

In the end, the World Bank experience was Mike's quasi-PhD in Culinary Arts. During his time there, he was a featured chef at a Taste of the Nation charitable event in D.C., a rare accomplishment for someone whose restaurant wasn't open to the public. After the troubled teenage years, where most of the time he felt like a failure, Mike's culinary career was a rocket on a launchpad.

He loaded up his U-Haul, gave his mother a long hug, and began the cross-country drive to California.

CHAPTER 3

Life Without the Handbook

Life doesn't come with a manual. It comes with a mother.

December 1980. It was Christmas morning in northern Virginia. A light snow covered the ground in the modest suburban neighborhood, and a five-year-old boy stood alone in the hallway, listening for the sounds of his parents.

An only child, Mike had learned to contain his excitement. Already, he knew when to act like an adult and when it was okay to be a kid.

His mother, Karen, shuffled out in her bathrobe and kissed his head.

"Mom, can I go?" he asked timidly.

"Yes, Mike. Go see what Santa brought."

His father, Don Rypka, joined them in the family room, five o'clock shadow and a worn look on his face. Karen eyed her husband, but then turned to watch Mike tear open the large gift in the center of the floor.

"A play kitchen!" Mike said as the scraps of wrapping paper fell to the shag carpet. "Yessssss!"

His father flashed a look of disapproval before retreating to the kitchen, Bloody Mary in hand, but Mike kept his eyes on his new toy. Karen smiled as he opened the little oven. He considered the basket of wooden fruits and vegetables, his eyes, glassy with possibility. She could almost see it, neurons firing.

ANOTHER CHRISTMAS A COUPLE of years later. From the outside, everything looked the same—snow covered the ground outside the modest suburban house. Eight-year-old Mike stood in the kitchen. In front of him, silver mixing bowls of dough and a row of Christmas tins readied with parchment.

He and his mother were baking cookies for the neighborhood. Later, this would be one of his earliest memories in the kitchen. He and mom, together. Christmas music in the background. His careful hands shaking out just the right amount of sprinkles for the stocking-shaped cookies.

A neighbor knocked on the door, and his mother welcomed her inside. Mike gave her a cookie tin.

"Well, thank you, Mike." The neighbor smiled down at him. "I've been thinking about you two…all alone during this season," she said, her voice going sullen.

Karen Timmons flashed a pained look and stepped in. "We're fine. Busy actually," she said unconvincingly.

His mother, of course, was lying. They were not fine. His father's absence seemed to stretch over everything. It was ever-encroaching, like twilight in winter. He'd later learn to see his dad differently. To understand that his dad, too, had burdens he was carrying. The Vietnam War. The pressures of his professional life as a successful photojournalist. He'd documented President Reagan for gosh sakes. But at the time, young Mike didn't know all that. It just seemed like his dad was skipping out on them, compounding Mike's feeling that nothing would ever be right. That he himself would never be right.

Mike excused himself just as his mother was pouring the afternoon tea. He slipped into the dark garage, stepping around his father's belongings which, if they hadn't been thrown out, were relegated to the garage. Mike opened the minifridge. Without thinking, he grabbed a can and shotgunned his first beer.

WHILE THE LITTLE WOODEN kitchen Mike got for Christmas that year was a productive first "play" with food, as Mike got into middle school, he had a few other encounters that weren't the case.

One afternoon in the school cafeteria, he helped incite a culinary brawl. A full-on food fight. Hotdogs and applesauce literally hitting the principal in the face like you see in the movies. The fiasco was enough to get Mike banned from attending his own sixth-grade graduation.

As innocent as a sixth-grade food fight sounds, it was just the tip of the iceberg. During his short preadolescence, Mike had transformed from a compliant little boy into a bitter, trouble-making kid. More than once, he'd been caught with cigarettes in the boys' bathroom. He acted like he was just curious about them, but he'd actually been smoking for years. It started sometime after his mom sent him down to the convenience store with a few dollars and a note for him to buy her a pack of Benson & Hedges.

Soon, he was able to secure some smokes for himself. Even his own preference. "My uncle's in town, and he likes Marlboros," Mike said. "Can I get a pack of those too?"

Mike was also drinking regularly. He had a couple of older buddies who helped with the supply of whatever it was at the time, and he'd even found ways to get some pot—someone's older brother, a neighborhood kid. From his early addictions he learned a simple truth about life: If you're looking for it, you can find it. Even as an 11-year-old kid.

Things had grown tense with his mom at home. She tried to be patient, but it was harder and harder to understand why her son had become such a delinquent. Karen Timmons was an academic and a professional journalist. She'd made a name for herself as a female newspaper editor in a man's world. Her son's ban from his sixth-grade graduation was the last straw. "I'm sending you to a military school two hours south of D.C.," she said matter-of-factly. "You've left me no choice."

The drive to Fork Union Military Academy was quiet. Mike stared out the window as the suburbs gave way to the wide green fields of central Virginia. Cows grazed in front of the grand, white-columned plantations that looked like he'd imagined them in the days of Thomas Jefferson.

But the openness, instead of helping him breathe, only made him feel panicked.

"We don't have to do this," he said to his mother, desperation mounting.

"I've given you all the chances in the world, Mike. But you can't go on like this. The kids you're hanging out with…they're just bad influences."

This was his personality sleight of hand. Even though he was at the epicenter of wrongdoing, he could still seem like the good kid. The one who just "fell in with the wrong crowd." Sometimes he was tempted to tell his mother that his friends weren't the instigators—*it was him*. He was the one who never felt settled in his own skin.

"I don't think the military is for me," he said. "I mean, look at what it did to dad."

His mother gripped the wheel at the mention of her ex-husband. "It was your grandad's idea. He thinks you need structure. And role models."

"Grandad lives in Ohio," Mike scoffed. "How does he know what I need? When dad comes back..."

"He's not coming back, Mike," his mother snapped. "I hired an investigator a while ago. Your dad's in Argentina. He has another life..." She reached a shaky hand into her purse and fumbled around for a cigarette. She cranked the window down.

Mike let the news sink in, the compounding sense of abandonment almost pressing him down into the passenger seat. It was like life had given everyone else a handbook, but somehow, it had left him out.

He gritted his teeth, mind swirling. *From now on, I'm going to fend for myself.*

The thought was like a promise. A stake in the ground.

FORK UNION WAS ABOUT what you'd expect from a military school founded in 1898 by a retired Baptist minister. In Mike's memory, his first few hours there were something like the opening scene in *Full Metal Jacket*. His suitcase was taken from him. His T-shirt and blue jeans traded for a starchy uniform. He followed a pack of skinny preteen boys to the barbershop to have his head shaved.

After only a few minutes on campus, he couldn't imagine that these were the role models his grandfather had hoped for him. Everyone seemed angry. "Attention!" one of them screamed.

Mike didn't know what "attention" was, but the dimple-chinned commander was quick to teach him. Mike looked down at his combat boots. They were shiny and laced so tight they rubbed at his ankles. He wanted a cigarette, but he settled for drinking a bottle of mouthwash later that night.

It wasn't long before he realized there were others at Fork Union like him. Those with addictions. The students weren't supposed to have a court record, but the truth was the school was unapologetically a place to put troublemakers. The boys, who might have been good-hearted, but couldn't stop partying. This made for an unspoken understanding between them—they, in their current states, were not wanted at home.

The restrictions made it harder to obtain any sort of contraband, but it was definitely not impossible. A few harbored cigarettes or cough syrup, and then there was the occasional liquor bottle someone could snag from a hotel while on leave. They took turns obtaining what was needed and always shared the spoils.

One of the few nice surprises from the school was Mike's own academic intelligence. At the academy, he was making the best grades he'd ever made in his life. Still, no matter how hard he tried, he couldn't do what was expected of him. Every day, he grew angrier that he'd been left there, and this manifested itself in different ways of bucking the system.

From the first day, the demerits rolled in. While the other kids were in the Mess Hall eating dinner, Mike marched until he had blisters on his feet. Everything about military school—particularly for boys just entering adolescence—was open and raw. Façades weren't only common, they were essential for self-preservation. The showers didn't have curtains, the bathrooms didn't have doors. The lack of privacy was so intense and the teasing so prevalent that you toughened up—or got crushed.

Mike hardened his attitude just to get by, and that only brought more trouble with authority. A stack of demerits meant no weekends away, and if you got enough of them—no visitors. Every month, the demerits were removed, and the slate wiped clean, but it wasn't a full week before he'd have lost all privileges again. Then it was back to marching punishment or "P.D." drills. Twelve hours was his longest, with a 10-pound rifle over his shoulder. Firing pins removed, of course.

Although the forced discipline didn't really stick, there were two takeaways from Fork Union that would stay with him always: irreverence and aversion to authority. He was marked by them, so much so that they would become cornerstones in the work culture that he would one day create.

Sometimes he stayed out of trouble enough to be granted a day visit from a friend or relative. It was too far for his mom to travel for just a few hours, but his aunt came over from Richmond. He wanted to be happy around her, but after just a few minutes, their conversations were bathed in his sulking and despair. "I just wanna get out of here."

Then, one day, he did.

The academy was a financial burden on his single mother, so after two years, she announced that he would not be returning. He finished up the year and came home to D.C., an eighth grader now, more muscular and worldly wise. He returned to public school, the chorus resounding in his head: *I'm freeeeee.*

Released from the boarding school restraints, Mike rocketed into the party life, and his drug and alcohol use reached new heights.

He had delivered newspapers on his bike when he was 8 years old, but he got his first real job after military academy—a fry cook at Popeyes. At 13, he was technically too young to work, so he lied on his application. He wanted his mom to think he could be responsible with his free time, but the truth was he needed the money to party.

In the afternoons, he rode the bus to the local mall, slipped on an apron, and stood, staring blankly over the vat of hot grease. He soon found that a chicken basket plunking into oil all day was a lot more entertaining if you were high.

At home, he was able to sober up just enough to keep up appearances for his mom. At the time, crack was an epidemic in D.C. Even Mayor Marion Barry had been caught smoking crack cocaine during an FBI sting. Mike watched the local news with his mother, as was their nightly tradition. She shook her head, disgusted, as the footage showed Mayor Barry in the grainy undercover footage.

"How could these guys do this kind of thing?" Mike chimed in, feigning disbelief.

He was a chameleon outside the home as well. Occasionally he'd go downtown to meet a dealer. On the way home from Capitol Hill, he'd use his mother's press badge to hop the secret subway. High as a kite, he'd have delightful conversations with the politicians and senators. He could see on their faces what they thought about him— *standup kid.*

But in high school, the façade began to crumble when Mike began smoking crack. A naturally gifted athlete, he was a starting defensive end on the football squad and a pitcher on the baseball team. But crack is the kind of drug that refuses to be recreational. It commands more and more of your time. So naturally, Mike's school attendance plummeted. He showed up for his first class, if at all, and then left to get high. He cleared the answering machine of the messages from the school secretary before his mom got home from work. He collected his "skip notices" and tossed them in the tall bushes in front of the house around the corner from his.

It wasn't long before his paycheck from Popeyes was nowhere close to supporting his habit, so he found ways to supplement it—stealing. His friend's parents owned a music store, so he and a couple of guys would swipe instruments and pawn them, and the little extra they could procure would be enough to keep them going.

Crack is often obtained on credit. But the goodwill between dealer and customer eventually runs out. Mike found this out when he was walking in his suburban Fairfax neighborhood one afternoon and a car rolled up beside him and a guy jumped out. "Are you Mike?" the man asked.

"Yeah, why?"

He pulled a handgun from his pocket in broad daylight. "Get on your knees."

"What are you talking about?" Mike slumped to the asphalt.

"You owe me $2,000."

"Who the hell are you, man? I don't owe you nothing!"

"You owe my cousin $2,000…which means you owe *me* $2,000. When are you going to pay up?"

"I…I don't know, man," Mike fumbled.

"Open your mouth." The man plunged the barrel between Mike's lips.

"Okay," Mike mumbled. "I'll get it."

"You've got two days…or I'm going to come find you."

Back home, Mike tore through the house. When he'd gotten behind with dealers in the past, he'd always been able to figure it out. He'd steal some money from his mom here and there. Cash his meager paychecks, borrow from a friend. But nothing he could come up with would be anywhere close to two grand. He began to panic, fumbling through the filing cabinet in his mother's house, looking for an old checkbook, something he could forge for cash.

And then, he found it. An absolute lifeline. The folder was labeled *College*, and as he scanned the pages inside, he could hardly believe his eyes—$25,000 worth of savings bonds.

He tucked the folder under his arm and raced out the door to the bank.

HIS FUTURE SECRETLY CASHED and his debts temporarily relieved, Mike went back to his old habits as though nothing had happened. This time, he even had some extra cash to burn.

Now that Mike was in good standing again, his dealer even let him in on a robbery he was planning—a string of convenience stores.

"We'd be set. We could move to Florida. Live on the beach," the dealer said.

Mike declined, but only after seriously considering it.

One day in spring, after the neighbor around the corner pruned his hedges, there was a knock on Mike's front door. His mother went to get it, and there, waiting for her, were the skip notices piled up in a neat stack as thick as an encyclopedia. His mother picked up the notices, tears welling in her eyes as she processed what they were.

"Forty-five days? You haven't been to school in *forty-five days?*" she said.

Mike saw the agony on her face and could say nothing. Whether she was in denial or just oblivious, she truly hadn't known how bad things had gotten, but suddenly, there it was, right in front of her.

She flipped through the notices, saying the dates aloud. All of it—the lying, the depth of deceit—could only add up to one thing.

"You're getting drug tested. Tomorrow," she said.

Mike said nothing but trudged back to his room.

She can't know. It will break her heart that I'm doing crack. His thoughts came in a stream of panic.

There was no choice but for him to bolt. His friend had tickets to a Grateful Dead concert coming up. He could follow the tour, making grilled cheese sandwiches. He could take care of himself on the road.

To a drug-addicted teen, this actually seemed like a plan. Anything to avoid hurting his mom. The weight of the single mother-son complex was always on his shoulders: *Dad let her down so much, I can't do it too.*

But then, when he was sure his only option was to run, something stopped him. *Just take the test,* a voice inside him said.

The next day, as Mike waited the few hours for the results of his drug test, he prayed for a miracle. But the verdict was just as expected: LSD, pot…crack.

He was loaded. With everything.

For whatever reason, his mother decided to give him a second chance. The outpatient treatment center was nonnegotiable, but she agreed not to send him to inpatient if he could work on himself and get clean.

He'd been born with the kind of physical frame that begged to be an athlete, but he'd shriveled down to a buck fifty, and he looked more like 12 than 15 as he pushed through the doors of his first group meeting. He poured coffee into a Styrofoam cup and pulled a cold metal folding chair up to the circle of men and women who had gathered. He looked around at their faces—most of them middle-aged, some much older than that. None of them kids.

Even in this supposed place of healing, he felt strange. Unwelcome. Years later, he would say this feeling was unusual for these kinds of meetings, but every once in a while, a group can give off a bad vibe.

One of the older men leaned in. "This place is for people with real problems." He studied Mike, a look of cool condescension on his face. "I've spilled more than you've drank in your lifetime, kid."

Mike pulled his hoodie tight around his chest as the creed professing God's help droned in the background.

If there was help, why wouldn't it ever reach him?

CHAPTER 4

The Birth of Opportunities

"If you come to a fork in the road, take it." (Attributed to Yogi Berra.)

Lafayette, Louisiana, 1992: Outpatient worked for a while. Worked in the sense that Mike didn't accidentally overdose, and he kept everyone around him just satisfied enough not to send him off anywhere.

In his heart, he wanted help. He was finally at a place where he was trying to get off the coke, but he thought he could still handle beer and the occasional blunt. So, he continued the dance, each day trying a little harder. With each failure, he confessed to his support group, each time more contrite and more ready to change than before.

But as he would admit years later, "Cocaine had me by the short hairs." The culmination of this truth came one evening in a neighborhood sewer when he dropped the last of his stash into the water. That moment, as he was crying into the murky river of sewage, he didn't just see his own desperate reflection, he saw his very soul.

It was enough. That night in the sewer, he gave up crack for life.

But as is often the case, if you stamp out one fire, others flame up. He'd cut off the head of the beast, but alcohol and pot use only took its place. He was off crack, so he thought that would be enough for everyone to just leave him alone. The counselors at the outpatient center were patient, kind even. Still, they would challenge him. "Mike, you keep saying you can stop, so stop. Why do you keep pissing dirty?"

"I can do this," he'd say to the assigned counselor, but really, he was talking to himself. He'd take a desire chip from the meeting. All night, he'd squeeze it in the palm of his hand, giving himself a pep talk: *I will not drink tomorrow.*

But the next morning, by 8:00 AM, he'd be drunk again. There was no alcohol left in the house, but it didn't matter. There was always a way: walk into a gas station, tuck a bottle into your jacket, walk out.

He slid by for more days and weeks, until one day in tenth grade, he showed up to school after he'd spent the morning downing a case of beer. The security guards must have been waiting for him, because as soon as he stepped onto school property, they descended and detained him until his mom showed up.

"Get her out of here!" Mike screamed. He was so embarrassed by the disappointment on his mother's face that he didn't know what to do other than to cuss her out.

A police officer appeared in the doorway of the principal's office, and Mike continued his stream of cursing.

"We've heard enough from you." The cop clamped down the handcuffs.

The officer's recommendation was to give Mike a little jail time. *Shake the kid up.*

But his mother pleaded his case. "He's a good kid. He's in outpatient treatment right now. It's just not enough."

The officer wasn't convinced, so after a long sigh, Mike's mother offered an alternative: "I'll put him in inpatient."

At the mention of that, Mike immediately sobered up. A full-time treatment center would be military school all over again. Or worse.

The officer nodded in agreement. "It's either that or a jail cell," he said.

In his memory, they went straight from the Fairfax police station to a rehab facility in Charlottesville, Virginia, without even stopping off at home to grab his bags.

The program was for 30 days, and thanks to the severe restraints (it was a lockdown facility), Mike managed to truly get sober for the first time since he was an eight-year-old kid.

A month later, his mother came down from D.C. to drive him to the halfway house the institute had recommended down in Louisiana.

Mike had stopped asking questions about what was next for him. He didn't want to know. He looked up at the building and grunted, amused. The name of the place was Opportunities.

At Opportunities, Mike, just 31 days clean, felt somewhat like a hostage.

Part of the goal of the halfway house was to integrate you back into society (without the temptations of your old associations and friends), so Mike found himself back in high school. But freedom is also a dangerous drug, and just the taste of it was enough to tip the scales again. Even at the halfway house, Mike had enough freedom to turn back to his old ways: drinking, popping pills, smoking a little pot when he could get it.

His days in Lafayette were spent, not working on getting clean, but planning to escape. A couple of times, he actually succeeded in running away. But homeless and alone at barely 16, he found himself way out of his depth. Roughed up by thugs in places darker and more dangerous than he'd ever imagined.

Louisiana might have been several hours from Fairfax, but word of Mike's abject indifference towards treatment eventually traveled back to his mother, so she made yet another hard decision. In two weeks, she would come and get him. No, it was not the rescue he was hoping for. She'd be escorting him from rehab to prison. "I'll be damned if I let you back out on the street again," she said.

Mike immediately went from apathy to utter despair. He hadn't been too interested in forging relationships with the other people at the halfway house, but his desperation must have been apparent, because suddenly, a few guys around him were concerned and wanting to help.

"Just try praying," one of them told him on the porch one afternoon.

"That's hocus pocus bullshit, man," Mike grunted. "If there's a God out there, he certainly hasn't had my back."

But that afternoon, Mike stopped in the middle of a field on the two-acre property. "I don't really even believe you're out there," he prayed, "and I don't know why I'm even doing this, but I'm hurting… and I need help."

He continued walking around the grounds, praying. When the sun set, he went back to his room and slept.

There was no bright light—no earthquake—but the next day, he woke up and something had changed.

"You look better today," one of the guys said at breakfast the next morning.

"You're not gonna believe this, but I tried it," Mike said. "I tried praying."

"And?"

"I feel better than I have in months. Better than I felt when I took my first drink."

The guy smiled. "Told you."

"My mom's still coming. And I'm probably going to jail in a few days, but I just have this weird feeling…like everything is going to be okay for once."

It was the first moment in his life he could remember feeling free. Free from anger. From addiction. From the weight of blaming his parents for the choices he made. There was peace in taking ownership, and prayer had brought him to that place.

During his time at Opportunities, Mike hadn't cared much about what was going on with the guys back home in Virginia. He knew everyone in his treatment team would support the decision to cut ties with his dealer and the guys he'd get high with. Still, occasionally, one of the boys would call, just to catch up.

"You didn't hear?" one of his buddies said on the phone one afternoon. "They did it. They actually did that robbery they were planning. Hit something like seven stores…the last of them was a 7-11 and somebody got killed. Two of them got 20 years, and one's supposed to get the chair."

Mike hung up the phone, his face almost numb from the news. That could have been him. That *would* have been him if he'd stayed back home.

"Thank you," he whispered, once again, nodding to the divine serendipity that saved his butt.

A few days later, his mom showed up, just as planned. Mike greeted her with a sincere smile and even a kiss. His bags were packed, and though he was deeply saddened by the plan, for once, he wasn't going to fight it.

"Sweetheart," his mom said cautiously. "I was talking with your counselor Ronnie, and he says something has changed in you."

"Oh yeah?" Mike's eyes lit up.

"He thinks you're finally ready to get better. He suggested you stay. Do you want to stay?"

Mike could barely contain his excitement. "Do I want to stay here instead of going to jail? Yes, Mom, I do. Besides, things really are different this time. I feel better, and I want to keep feeling better."

Mike's mother sighed. Inside, she was tired, even skeptical, but she gave him a tight hug and walked back to her car alone.

A few months later, more good news: Mike graduated from the rehab program and his counselors thought he was ready to go home. He waved goodbye to Opportunities, not knowing that years down the road this name—this very idea—would become a cornerstone in his business empire.

WHEN MIKE CAME BACK, he was in the middle of his junior year of high school in Fairfax. With a new attitude and the proper support group in place, he was flourishing. He'd started to meet others who were young and also in recovery. He didn't feel so alone.

But not all of the kids in recovery were serious about getting well, and one night, after one of them offered him some mushrooms, Mike slipped up. Seven months of sobriety down the drain. Suddenly, again it seemed the road was too long and too hard.

What if I just quit worrying about it? The Grateful Dead are coming back to town again. I could follow the band…sell things to take care of myself.

But something told him to go to his meeting that night and just confess. The shrooms, the music, the easy path—they would be waiting in the morning.

So, he did. He stood in front of the group and told the room what had happened, and they received him with open arms. There, at that meeting in April 1992, he picked up a desire chip for the last time.

The lifelong battle that followed was just that—a battle. As Mike would later explain, "That one night off the wagon kicked the cravings back full force. I hadn't really been struggling before that, but one day back at the old habits, and every day the following year was a fight to stay clean."

Mike knew he needed to utilize every resource in the support system, so he got a sponsor. And every time Mike sat in his car outside of the 7-11, staring into the drink cooler at the bottles of beer, he called Joel. And each time, after 20 minutes of talking, he didn't want to drink anymore.

Sobriety battle aside, Mike also had the challenges of a normal teenage kid. First and foremost: he hadn't graduated high school yet. He realized how much easier it was to keep your grades up when you actually went to class. Since he was coping okay and his grades this time were decent, his mother thought it would be all right if he looked for some part-time work. So he tried his hand at a restaurant job. This time, he expanded his culinary base and took a position as a busboy at Le Peep, a popular breakfast joint.

Things were going pretty well. He showed up on time. He bussed the tables happily and efficiently. He fell in love with the pace of a busy restaurant—the energy of it. He didn't mind being on his feet. During breakfast and weekend brunches, when service seemed like an indoor sprint, he could just turn off his brain and work. It was a good rhythm for him. The daily repetition of mundane tasks was like laying track for who he was going to be.

But then, one Saturday morning, half of the kitchen crew didn't show up. After 30 minutes of making phone calls and banging around pots and pans, the manager called Mike back into the dishpit.

"Rypka, haven't you worked in a kitchen?"

"No. I mean…I fried chicken at Popeyes," Mike said hesitantly. "But I don't know if that counts…"

"It'll have to. Come on."

The manager positioned Mike in front of the grill. "You just need a few basics and you'll be fine. Here's how we do the bacon," he said as the meat popped and sizzled. "And the potatoes need to look like this…"

The crash course was over in less than five minutes. "Got it?" the manager said as he went to unlock the door for the guests already lined up outside.

The shift, according to Mike, was a total shitshow. Food barely made it onto the plates. Just as Mike set one order in the hot window, the printer spit out five more tickets.

But he held his own. After the rush was over, a couple of servers came up to him to thank him for stepping in. "Hey, you saved us today," one of them said.

It was the first time in a long time that he could remember being the star of the day. Like he'd come through for someone. He'd had that feeling before—mostly in football—but the drugs had long taken it away. It felt good to work towards a common goal, to bust ass with a team again.

The manager also congratulated Mike and gave him an instant promotion. "How would you like to be done with the dishes? Wanna try out line cook?"

"Sounds like fun," Mike said.

One of the cooks took Mike under his wing, and eventually, Mike learned every position in the kitchen. The job gave him structure, money, and even a few new friends. The breakfast joint usually had an hour, even two-hour, wait on Saturdays, and the fast pace offered him something that was crucial in his recovery: "It helped me turn off the old thinker."

The restaurant world had its hooks in him pretty deep, but after a year and a half at Le Peep, Mike decided to branch out once again. He went out on a limb and got a job at the Springfield Golf and Country Club not too far from his house. Everything about working there was a step up, from the menu to the crisp chef coats. It felt like the bigtime, but it was intimidating.

Thanks to his experience at Le Peep, Mike could keep up with the line, but when it came to some foundational skills—like how to properly use a knife—it was clear he didn't have his chops yet. The head chef of the country club, Chef Bryan Dolieslager, was in a different league than the cooks Mike had worked with in chain restaurants. While Mike didn't consider his new boss unkind, Bryan was definitely impatient. He didn't have time for hand holding, and after Mike had spent a couple of weeks struggling with basic skills, Bryan made it clear that he wasn't impressed.

Mike could see the writing on the wall. He could sense it every time he fumbled up in the kitchen, but he wasn't ready to give up just yet. He wanted to learn. "I know you are not thrilled with my performance," Mike said to Bryan one afternoon, "and you're probably ready to fire me by now, but I like it here. And I can work harder, if you could just give me a second chance."

"Two weeks," Bryan said, not looking up from his chopping. "You've got two weeks to prove you can keep up."

The grace period Bryan extended him (and the unspoken affirmation that went along with it) were all Mike needed to take off. Before long, he had proven himself to be a worthy sous-chef. Bryan started asking Mike to do banquets and buffets with him, and soon, the senior in high school found himself heading up catering events. On those busy nights, Mike got to experience the whole gamut of his creation: from prepping to cooking to presentation on the plate. It was satisfying and more fun than he'd ever had (outside of partying).

"How about I start calling you my banquet manager?" Bryan asked him one night.

"Is that what I am now? Officially?" Mike asked.

"Looks like it to me," Bryan said.

The new responsibility did wonders for Mike and furthered his love for the culinary world. The only problem was the lifestyle required late nights and weekends. It also meant exposure to booze—good booze—and lots of it. He stuck it out a few months, but ultimately, Mike realized that while he was having the time of his life, he wasn't sure it was worth his life. So as high school graduation approached, he kept working at the country club but started looking for the next thing. His passion was in cooking, but his sobriety still meant more to him than anything.

A natural path for many people who've been through treatment is substance abuse counseling, so Mike thought he might give it a try. He enrolled in a four-year program at a community college. It wasn't a bad fit. He'd always been great with people—all types of people—and he hoped he could use his personal experience to provide opportunities for those on the brink.

He was halfway into the first semester in the counseling program when he attended a career day at the college. He spent the majority of his time at the tables designated for social work, but something caught his eye and he drifted over to the hospitality section of the gymnasium. And there, right in front of him, was a culinary institute. He walked over to the table, the banner in front read: Johnson & Wales. He didn't really talk to anyone, but he shoved a couple of flyers into his backpack, just in case.

That night, in the middle of the night, he sat up in bed. He turned his light on and went to his backpack and pulled out the flyers for the institute. He flipped through them, his heart soaring. Then, a thought came into his head like lightning, clear as day. *What are you doing? You should be a chef.*

But he was doing well in the counseling program. For once, he had a real plan, and he was going to stick to it. He turned the light off and laid back down, but still, he couldn't shake the excitement. It was too much to sleep. It was clear to him at that moment—what he was feeling was a sign.

It was the longest night of his life, but he managed to hold off until morning before he came barreling out of his room with his news.

"Mom, I'm dropping out of school. I know what I'm supposed to do now. I'm going to be a chef."

His mother looked up from her morning newspaper, not even slightly amused. "Like hell you are."

"Mom, I'm serious. It's so clear now. I'm in a good place. I'm strong enough to do this, and it's truly my passion—it's what I'm supposed to do."

"Tell you what. Finish the semester. Then we can go visit some culinary schools. Just give it a little time to make sure this is what you want to do."

"Thank you, Mom! Thank you." Mike almost picked her up from the breakfast table in a hug. "You'll see. This is going to be amazing."

CHAPTER 5

From Culinary to Enron

Learn what you can and get out.

Miami, 1994: After interviewing at Johnson & Wales in Miami, Mike went back to the country club and broke the news to Bryan.

"You think it's a good idea?" Mike asked.

"Lots of restaurants. Lots of options down there. And you can get some sun. We'll miss you, buddy."

"Might come back here when I finish," Mike offered.

"I hope not."

"Huh?"

"Don't get me wrong," Bryan said. "I'd always take you back, but if I can give you one piece of advice, it's this—*don't stay anywhere long.*"

When you get out—for the next six to eight years—learn what you can and then move on to the next place."

"But I thought I should show consistency."

"Maybe in the program, but not as a chef. You need to be exposed to as many different ways of doing things as possible. Spend no more than two years in any one kitchen, and gracefully move on—but get your next job before you leave."

Mike was working so hard to stay consistent and steady that, at the time, the advice didn't really make sense. "Okay," he said, not fully convinced, but he never forgot what Bryan said.

IN MIAMI, EVERYTHING WAS new. Not just the Johnson & Wales campus, which had only been open about a year, but the sensory experience was like viewing the same old world in a new spectrum of color—the flowers, the music, the spices. Flavors seemed richer and everything seemed enhanced by the heat.

Mike excelled in the culinary program, and after two years, he graduated on time and continued his education down the street, focusing on Hospitality Management at Florida International University. During his coursework (and afterward) Mike remembered and began applying Bryan's advice. He did everything from kosher catering to shucking oysters at the Chart House before settling in at the popular five-star eatery, Mark's Place in Ft. Lauderdale. The restaurant, with a blend of traditional and tropical styles, was known for pushing the envelope. At Mark's, Mike began his unofficial apprenticeship in flavor and color.

The chef, Mark Militello, a native of Buffalo, New York, had earned a name for himself, using the resources of the Caribbean (without being bound to them) and elevating the dining in South Florida to the level of more established places on the West Coast.

Mark's innovations meant that Mike was always finding something new on the big white dinner plates, from fried calamari on a pizza (before anyone dreamed those kinds of combinations were possible for pizza) to oak-fired rotisserie duck and squid-ink pasta. The artistry (and the unusual flavor palates) didn't go unnoticed by the public or the press. Mark's received national write-ups and the reputation of being one of the premier restaurants in the region. There was also a year and a half waitlist to be a server there, because waiters were making $100,000 a year.

Though Mike wasn't a star player on the culinary team just yet, he learned something just from being in the huddle. As the menu changed daily, there was a chef's meeting before each shift to get everyone on the same page. Mike was in charge of sauté and frying appetizers. He helped with prep and pizzas and sometimes manned the rotisserie station. As Mike would later remember, "This was back in the day when you had to have thick skin to work in a kitchen. Yelling was common. So was the occasional pot being thrown around if you did something wrong. Sous chefs were tasting sauces over your shoulder, making you start from scratch if they weren't just right."

But Mike took the critique (and occasional verbal scolding) he received at Mark's as part of his fine-dining boot camp. He learned what he could from one restaurant, then moved on to the next thing. One of those opportunities was working at the South Beach Food and Wine Festival. There, Mike got his first taste of chef-driven food events. He was enamored with possibility.

He then began working on Fisher Island, the elite little Miami Beach community that's known for having the highest income per capita of any place in the United States. On the island, Mike worked alongside White House–caliber chefs. He picked up some classic, foundational techniques, making and serving everything from consommés to aspics. The culmination of his time on the island was his role of *garde-manger* at the Organization of American States, a summit meeting event that included an eight-course meal for then-President Clinton and other elite political leaders. Today, when thinking back on the event, Mike jokes, "I was part of the garnish team back at a time when every plate had a garnish and every garnish had a garnish." The eye was a huge part of the dining experience, and it was common for fruits and vegetables to be carved and crafted in creative ways.

All the while, the Secret Service stood post in the kitchen looking on, even escorting the staff to the restrooms and back. As the dessert course was being finished, Mike decided that 16 hours was enough for one day, so he tried to get a head start on the commute home, but it still took an hour and a half to get off the island with all the checkpoints. He watched the helicopters whirring overhead and the Navy SEAL boats bobbing in the distance, and he thought about his commanders in military school, if they could see him now. How far he had come from the lonely kid—an outcast, a delinquent—to serving the President of the United States.

SOUTH BEACH, WITHOUT QUESTION, left its mark. Culinary school aside, Miami itself made Mike fall in love with street food, it piqued his interest in cultural fusion, and it forever hooked him on big flavor and spice. "I mean, you're more Cuban than I am," a friend from culinary school joked with him. "You are obsessed with plantains."

Mike took a couple of smaller positions as well; one he remembers with particular humor and humility—the Shiner's Club in Hollywood, Florida—the only restaurant job that ever fired him. It was just a Friday gig, but the problem was he could never get access to the kitchen until noon. Most days that was no big deal, but there was the one time—the big Shiner's event—where they were serving corned beef. Dinner was at 6:00 PM, which meant to get the food on the plate, he'd have to cook the meat twice as fast as he wanted to.

The result?

"I fucked up the corned beef. Tough as leather," Mike later said. "I got fired that night. But I learned something big. Don't sign up for something that's not possible."

After culinary school and some respectable roles in real kitchens, Mike was wondering what was next. He decided it was time to go back home to Virginia. And there, after the World Bank had officially jet started his corporate career, he realized once again he couldn't stay. Like an early explorer, he knew there was more out there waiting for him, so he said the hard goodbyes and moved cross-country to California.

While in Los Angeles, in addition to MTV, Mike assumed other corporate dining leadership roles for titans within the Marriott realm: Walt Disney Animation Studios in Burbank and the newly opened Interscope Records. At Interscope, he helped set up their international café, all the while honing the skill of multi-unit management.

Hollywood, California, was fun, exciting. It felt relevant. A far cry from the Hollywood, Florida, he'd left. Someone was always working on a flashy new project and there was always something interesting to talk about.

In California, Mike also got a chance to be on the other side of the chopping block, serving as a culinary trainer (a role that allowed him to teach international cooking classes for big corporations). Most chefs know how to cook French food, maybe a little Italian, but not Ethiopian or Moroccan. Thanks to his experience at the World Bank, Mike, at age 24, found himself with some real depth as far as international cuisine was concerned. The chefs would come in the door knowing what Szechuan chicken was supposed to taste like, but they'd never had it prepared by someone who was Chinese. But Mike had.

The teaching was rewarding, and once again Mike found himself leading and instructing those who were twice his age. But glitz and glam aside, in L.A., Mike felt the rumblings of homesickness. After two and a half years in California, he was weary of life in Los Angeles, but he wasn't actively looking to relocate until he got a call from an old friend at the World Bank.

"You want me to come to Houston?" Mike asked. "Texas?"

"Yeah, I know it's a shift in mindset," the manager said.

"Cowboys and rednecks…I'd say so."

"Just think about it, you'd be the head chef. In charge of all the hiring, menu design. It's your dream job...this is a *massive* Marriott account."

"But for Enron? Those guys are super corporate."

"Yeah, and they're killing it in stocks. They're basically handing out blank checks. It's a carte blanche—trust me."

WHEN MIKE ARRIVED IN Texas, Enron had already completed one tower in Houston and was working on a second. The state-of-the-art kitchen had already been finished and they needed Mike to develop a cutting-edge café menu. It was going to be a calling card for Sodexo (the French food services and facilities management company that had merged with Marriott and was running the Enron show).

And as soon as Mike arrived, Enron representatives affirmed what his buddy had said: "We'll pay for whatever—just make it good. Spare no expense!"

Four months into taking a position, Mike found himself in charge of a world-class kitchen and catering facility, an army of new hires, and at the beginning of the most promising job of his life.

Then, the news broke.

That morning was just like any other. Mike went into work as usual, but one of the kitchen managers came rushing up as soon as he walked in the door. "I'm guessing you saw the news," he said.

"I'm not much of a news guy," Mike said casually. "What's up?"

"There was this huge scandal with Enron," he lowered his voice. "They've stolen a bunch of money…doesn't look good."

Mike was in total shock. He wasn't sure how to process this information, but he knew, at least for the time being, he had a kitchen to run. People would be looking to him to remain calm. "Well, I'm sure it will all get sorted out. In the meantime, we have work to do."

But that work would prove difficult. The days went on, and the Enron scandal began to unravel like one of Mike's mother's crocheted potholders. Suddenly, there were 30 news cameras outside the building every morning. Mike did his best to avoid them. "I don't know anything. I'm just the chef," he'd say if someone happened to shove a microphone in his face.

Though Mike and the rest of the employees only talked about it in whispers, it became clear to most of them that the Enron situation was like the *Titanic*. The ship was going down and everyone was frantically clambering to the top, waiting for a rescue boat…or to drown.

The layoffs went floor by floor. Each day during the two-week window, Mike and his team waited while the powers that be decided how many jobs they could absorb.

The end total: 32 positions would be saved. Since Mike was the new guy, the higher ups put him in charge of letting the other 80 people know the bad news.

In a cruel twist of fate, Mike sat at a desk in the gorgeous new café (that had yet to serve a single guest) and began firing the people he had brought on board to work for him.

One by one, they came in, following the one-hour time slots he'd assigned to them. "I'm so sorry, but I don't have a job for you," he'd say, trying to deliver the news empathetically but efficiently.

The weight was tremendous. Of course it wasn't his fault, but after looking into dozens of tearful faces, many of whom had wagered everything on *his* promise to give them an opportunity, Mike himself started to feel like a fraud. They'd left good jobs—even their homes and families—to work for a company as promising as Enron and its energetic young chef.

And it wasn't just the new hires that Mike had to let go. Mike found that they'd also sneaked some faithful employees onto his firing list—hourly workers who had been with Sodexo for years. It was a realization young Mike hadn't really experienced yet in his career: sometimes business is just business. He took it as a lesson, but it didn't come without a scar.

Needless to say, after Enron, Mike needed some time to decompress. He stayed in Houston and accepted a short gig at Hewlett-Packard, taking a month or so to freshen up their menu. From there, Marriott found him a more long-term position with Dell in Austin. He was in charge of all food service at 13 of their corporate locations, which was exciting in its own right, but even better than that, he fell in love with his quirky new hometown. Austin had all the heart of Texas but offered more originality than he'd experienced anywhere else in the country.

While Mike appreciated the stability of Dell after such a tumultuous ride at Enron, his time there also presented some challenges. The hyper-competitive environment meant that the company wanted to save every dollar it could on food costs. The translation: Mike was more a cook than a chef. Again, the words of Chef Bryan from the country club echoed in his ears: *learn what you can and get out.* At Dell, Mike's primary lesson was not so much from the kitchen as it was from conference calls—he had to learn how to manage managers. Being in charge of over a dozen sites was no small task, and young Mike once again found himself having to speak with more authority than his years suggested he had earned.

But after a couple years with Dell, Mike was disenchanted with the corporate grind and open to the next thing when he got a call from an old friend. Chuy's, the popular local Tex-Mex chain, was looking to open up a sister store and they wanted some menu input.

"Basically, they need a creative chef for the whole new venture," Mike's buddy pitched the job to him. "It's a 500-seater on lakefront property. I told him you're the most creative chef I know."

"Not sure that I am anymore," Mike said, almost to himself.

But the more he thought about it, the more the gig seemed like just what he needed. A creative shot in the arm. A chance to be an artisan again. Sure, it was definitely taking a leap. The corporate guys saw things in black and white, but (barring a scandal and impending collapse) those same guys paid the bills. Still, the more Mike thought about it, the more he realized that this was his chance to start doing his own thing. He didn't have a family to worry about yet; he didn't have kids. It was enchanting, the freedom to experiment with dishes again without the pressures of the almighty bottom line that had driven his corporate career for the last few years. And it didn't hurt that the restaurant was overlooking a lake.

"When do they want me to start?" he asked.

CHAPTER 6

The Taco Tour

What's in a name?

Lake Austin, Texas, 2004. Though the decision to join forces with Chuy's Tex-Mex was one that Mike never regretted, their new project, Lucy's Boatyard—the restaurant he was supposed to lead from conception to expansion—was like a flower that just wouldn't bloom. In their pitch to him, the owners had gotten one thing right: it was on "lakefront property"—but not much turned out as he'd expected when he said goodbye to Dell.

Still, Mike stayed with Lucy's for more than a year as the company tested concepts and tried to gain momentum. He worked closely with the owners as their creative chef, nudging them to decide what they wanted to be, aside from "a place that serves burgers and shrimp."

"I'll make whatever you want," Mike kept saying. "But you have to decide what it is you want."

Meanwhile, Mike spent time at the other stores owned by the company, visiting various Chuy's locations and the Hula Hut (the one-off restaurant next door to Lucy's). The Hula Hut was, and had always been, a big hit. Waterfront dining, fun drinks, kitschy décor were all part of the package deal with this Tex-Mex Hawaiian fusion. Mike was able to learn a lot by observation. The warmth and character that came with an individually owned and family-run business was refreshing to him, particularly after he'd spent so much time working for corporate giants under the Marriott umbrella. It was clear that the "Chuy's guys" (as he called the owners) loved Austin and wanted to be a part of keeping it cool and authentic. In fact, they'd snatched up the property on Lake Austin partly because they were terrified it would fall into the hands of a giant chain like Joe's Crab Shack.

Mike saw another reason for the success of the Chuy's team—they made good food, and because of that, he saw that the servers had a certain confidence when they brought the plates to the table. The company treated its employees well, therefore employee retention was high.

But despite the solid foundation, Lucy's was like a ship that never left the harbor. It had its good days, even weeks, but the 500-seat capacity restaurant was cavernous as hell. There could be 100 diners in there, happily enjoying their meals, and it would still seem like a slow night. They tried rearranging the furniture to make it feel more intimate, but that just confused the guests, and the problem of pervasive emptiness was left unsolved. (Particularly if you glanced next door and compared it with the always-bustling Hula Hut.)

Though it's a gamble to set up shop next to your own restaurant—
and therefore competing with yourself—Hula Hut itself wasn't really
the problem, but the mindset behind it was. Chuy's had been a success,
Hula Hut had also been a success, so of course the owners and investors
naturally assumed: *Whatever we do will be successful, because that's how
it's worked in the past.*

So, for the ambitious young chef, the shock waves that came from
Lucy's failure served as a good cautionary tale: *success doesn't just transfer
horizontally. You can use the same formula, but the experiment doesn't
necessarily work.*

But one good thing that did come out of the experience was the
friendship Mike found with kitchen manager Jay Wald. Jay had been
brought over by Chuy's to run the kitchen at Lucy's. Even though Jay
was just in his late 20s, he'd already been in the restaurant business for
almost a decade. Mike found in Jay an old soul. He was more ambitious
than most younger folks in the industry. Like Mike, while he didn't
mind doing the grunt work, Jay dreamed of bigger things.

Jay also found a kindred spirit in the kitchen. He recognized Mike's
passion for food and his commitment to his coworkers. Instead of assert-
ing himself and his authority, Mike valued people and their opinions,
regardless of their "rank" in the kitchen—a rare quality in someone with
Mike's credentials. Jay and Mike tag teamed the Lucy's project, all the
while daydreaming of going into business together one day.

"What if we did a breakfast concept?" Mike would say, pitching Jay
ideas. "That's one market I don't think Austin has nailed yet."

"Yeah, there's nothing out of the box anyway. There's also fast-casual salads. People want to eat healthier, but it has to be faster. It could be creative and build-your-own…"

The two continued this spitballing, but as the weeks and months went by and Lucy's kept performing poorly, it was clear—no matter how many adjustments they made—the restaurant just wasn't going to take.

After Lucy's officially shut down, the owners offered Mike and Jay positions at the Hula Hut, but Mike was done. Now almost 32, he was at a crossroads. He still didn't have a family. He'd worked so much, for so long, jumping straight from one role to the next. This was his window of opportunity. Jay, on the other hand, wasn't there yet.

"I gotta take the Hula job," Jay explained to Mike. "I'm not quite ready yet. You understand, right?"

"Of course I do, man," Mike said, "Hula Hut is a great restaurant. You'll do well there." Mike didn't fault his new friend for staying in the safe lane. Jay had a young wife, and even though Mike and Jay had mentally white-boarded some dreams, the tumultuous waters of going into business for yourself wasn't something you could push on someone else. But Mike realized deep in his bones it was finally time to do his own thing. He'd worked with enough people older than him to know that the door to taking these kinds of risks didn't stay open forever. The older you got, the more it started to close.

So Mike respectfully turned down the Hula Hut job and left the Chuy's team with no hard feelings. If he was honest, it had been a disappointment. The hopes for Lucy's were high and the role Mike had been offered in its development had seemed damn near perfect. But to Mike, crying over spilt milk seemed like a real waste of time. "Hardships have taught me, hey, if this goes down, I'll survive. Some of my greatest gifts have come out of my greatest disappointments."

Mike took a couple of weeks to plot his next move. He considered taking out a small loan and using it to travel. To see the world. He could be inspired and for once, really have the time to think about his profession. Isn't that what most kids his age had done in their 20s, while he'd been putting in 60-hour weeks? It seemed like the most plausible plan, until the night his buddy Bill pitched him a different idea.

"What if we opened up a taco truck?" Bill said.

"Tacos?" Mike laughed. "You can't throw a rock in Austin without hitting a taco stand."

"You've won the *Chronicle*'s hot sauce competition for two years in a row now. It's definitely something you could crush."

"Sure, but that doesn't mean the market needs more Mexican."

Bill was right about Mike's accolades. Just for fun, Mike had entered the *Austin Chronicle*'s Hot Sauce competition in 2004 and 2005 and won in the individual green sauce category both times. His three-chili and tomatillo sauce had created some serious buzz. And he'd made it using his crappy community apartment grill.

"What do you know about restaurants?" Mike asked.

"Nothing," Bill said. "But I know you're a good enough chef to have one."

That loyalty was the reason Bill and Mike were friends. The two were different as night and day, but Bill was an encourager and a dreamer. The kind of guy who could motivate you to change the world or get you in a mess of trouble.

"You gonna quit the landscaping biz to help me?"

"Nah. But I can help you run a business. And the best part is that you can have my grandfather's old trailer."

"That rusty piece of shit?" Again, Mike shook his head at the ridiculousness of the picture they were painting. "Does it even run?"

"I could pay for the reno…it'd be a free place to open up shop. Virtually no overhead."

"My first real kitchen in a roach coach? I don't know…" Mike shrugged, thinking.

At the time, serving food from a trailer was a market solely occupied by the *loncheras,* Latin food trucks that puffed and rattled their way from one construction site to the next. The locals called them by another name: roach coaches. At the time, the term "gourmet food truck" wasn't just unheard of, it was a complete oxymoron. Eating from a trailer was a quick, modest meal…reserved for those okay with the possibility of food poisoning.

But one thing about Bill's idea really struck a nerve: it was a way, albeit unorthodox, to get good food to the masses. It was also approachable. In all of Mike's dreaming and scheming, he'd never seen fine dining in his future. He'd done the white-tablecloth thing at the country club, Mark's Place, even freakin' Fisher Island, but if it was going to be authentically himself, his desire was simpler than that. He wanted an emphasis on street food, while still keeping it fresh, flavorful, and affordable.

"We should go on a tasting tour," Bill said. "We'll go around, eat the tacos that are already out there...figure out how you can make them better."

Mike thought for a minute. It wasn't the worst idea he'd ever heard. It beat sitting around trying to theoretically craft some formal "business model." (And given his experience in literally every facet of the restaurant business, he honestly didn't want anyone else's two cents.)

"You know, Bill, you may have a plan."

AFTER A FEW WEEKS of delicious research, Mike and Bill had gained a couple of pounds, eaten some good food, but were largely underwhelmed. Along their tour, they'd hit every big market in Texas: Dallas, Houston, San Antonio.

"Tacos in Texas are great—don't get me wrong. But it's all the same damn thing," Mike said. "Onions, cilantro, maybe a little cheese and a sauce...nothing fancy."

Based on this assessment, he landed on the framework for his restaurant: quality and affordability. Tacos that would be non-traditional—not Mexican or Tex-Mex.

"Here's what I'm thinking," Mike told Bill as they crossed over the Congress Avenue Bridge, the sun just beginning to set. "We're going to let the tortilla be the base and just have fun with the rest."

"You got it," Bill said. "We'll have the trailer ready next week."

Once they had the concept down, the next thing they needed was a name. The problem was everything they came up with sounded too Mexican. They wanted the flavor and the influence of the standard Tex-Mex, but even with the name, they wanted to let customers know that this was a significant twist.

The partners were talking it over one night, and Bill sat up in his chair. "I got it!"

"What?" Mike said.

"I've been beating my head against a wall because I had this name from a long time ago…I had kinda tucked it away, and I couldn't remember it…and I finally did," Bill said.

"So what is it?"

"It was way back in the 90s, and I was at late-night at Rosie's El Pastor, so I was kinda drunk…"

"What is the name?!"

"Torchy's."

"Torchy's," Mike said, turning it over in his head.

"I had this vision of an Airstream, with this red neon Torchy's sign…maybe a flame coming out of the Y."

"Dude, I think that's it."

CHAPTER 7

The Halloween that Saved the Tacos

You gotta spend money to make money.

Austin, 2006: If you ask him today, Mike will tell you it was passion and the sheer will not to fail that helped him muscle through the gauntlet of opening up shop.

But it was also something else: it was going to work, because *it had to work*. Mike had used every penny he had just to get his new business off the ground. To get the trailer fully "Torchified," as he and Bill said, he'd even taken out a loan on his house. He knew it was the right move at the right time, but still, it was a huge risk. The kind of pressure he felt is somewhat foreign to a lot of entrepreneurs starting out today. To the modern-day college grad with a business degree and a big SBA loan with months to repay. These MBA types, with all due respect, don't have the same amount of skin in the game. So they might not understand the guy who hopped on his Vespa and went wherever he had to, saying, "Try this taco so you will buy some later, dammit."

After their Fifth Street landlord axed the trailer's power cord due to "unpaid rent," Mike was left with no choice but to operate out of Bill's driveway. Serving food in a residential area could get them heavily fined or permanently shut down—but they didn't really have a choice. Mike kept his chin up, all the while confiding in Juan, "We're violating some serious health codes here, man."

With all the deliveries, Mike needed a runner. So he hired his second employee: a guy Bill knew named Dui (pronounced Dew-we). Dui was the first Torchy's delivery guy.

"Man, his name is kinda ironic for a driver, don't you think?" Bill pointed out.

While Dui was making deliveries on the Vespa, Mike spent the afternoons driving around, scouting potential trailer locations. He wanted to maintain a presence downtown, but that limited his choices. He'd seen a little snow cone trailer on the banks of Bouldin Creek off South First Street, but after a gentle inquiry about the landlord, the snow cone guys had shut him down. "There's no room here, buddy."

"Really?" Mike asked, looking around the empty gravel lot. It was vacant but for a picnic table and a firepit, and then left it at that.

A few days later, Mike passed by the Bouldin Creek spot again, and this time when he saw the same snow cone guys, instead of serving up customers, they were packing up. He looked closer and realized that they seemed to be dismantling their trailer. Permanently.

He whipped his Vespa into the gravel lot. After he again exchanged a few pleasantries, he cut to the chase. "Are you guys leaving?"

"Yep," one of them said. "We'll be gone by the end of the day."

"That's too bad," Mike said. "May I ask why?"

The guy laughed. "It's called money. Can't seem to make any."

"Well, do you think now you might be willing to give me the phone number for your landlord?" Mike said, hiding his excitement out of respect for their failure.

One of the guys reached in the trailer and ripped a sheet from the ticket book. "Here you go…but I don't know if he will rent to you or not."

The second location for the trailer, like the first, was less than ideal. The lot near the creek didn't exactly scream, "Stop and eat here!" But they had an honest-to-goodness lease on the space. It was on South First near Gibson Street, which, while it wasn't a main intersection, was a big thoroughfare for people from South Austin coming downtown.

"It's definitely a floodplain." Bill stood, hands on hips, surveying the u-shaped lot his partner had made great efforts to procure.

"Technically," Mike said. "But maybe that's a good thing. It'll keep people from building on it…"

"Like my grandad said, just wait and hope that the creek don't rise."

But to their surprise, Bouldin Creek on South First Street suited them, and soon they started to refer to it as the true birthplace of Torchy's.

"I think this spot needs a name," Mike said to Bill as they locked up one night. "How bout we call it the South Austin Trailer Park and Eatery?"

"Nice ring to it," Bill conceded.

Mike had a sign made, and lo and behold, the moniker stuck.

IN OUR MODERN WORLD, where constant scrolling has led to the popular medical diagnosis of "smartphone thumb," it's little wonder why businesses must fight to be heard. There's no place for the meek. No hope for shrinking violets. Mike instinctively understood this, and after muscling through September still barely breaking even, he was ready to do whatever it took to draw attention to his new company. Even if that meant using his own body as advertising. He ran the city-wide Keep Austin Weird 5K dressed as the Torchy's devil to draw attention to the brand. He crossed the finish line, decked out in red body paint and wearing an adult diaper. It was one thing he and Bill were in agreement on: use every resource you've got.

That is, until Bill got another one of his genius ideas.

It was a perfectly cool fall evening—a rarity for Austin in September—when an 18-wheeler pulling a load of Halloween pumpkins turned into the Torchy's lot. The driver got out and stretched, strolling over to the order window.

"What can I get for ya, man?" Mike said cheerily.

The guy slapped an invoice on the counter. "Well, I was supposed to be dropping off, but now that you mention it…I'm pretty hungry." He stepped back and stared at the menu.

"I'm sorry," Mike scanned the invoice, brow furrowing. "What do we owe ya for exactly?"

"Oh you've already paid. A fella named Bill ordered them last week," the driver said and nodded to his partner who was unhooking the massive trailer.

"Pumpkins?" Mike's face turned as red as Torchy himself. "Why would he order $12,000 worth of pumpkins when we're running a taco restaurant?"

The guy shrugged. "Probably need to ask him that."

"Stay right here for a minute please," Mike said, feigning calm as he stepped out of the back of the trailer and called his partner.

"Yello," Bill said, his tone jovial as usual.

"Bill, please, for the love of God, tell me that you didn't max out our last credit card on 44 pallets of pumpkins!"

"Oh, did they finally come?"

"Yes! And they're currently taking up the only parking we have for guests."

"Advertising," Bill said, unfazed. "It's a good investment."

"Did you also buy some magic freakin beans?" Mike said. "I don't think you're understanding how this works… *We need food in the trailer to serve customers!*"

"Gotta spend money to make money, Mike."

Mike clenched his teeth but held his tongue. He'd heard that phrase one too many times in their short partnership. "We'll talk about this later," Mike said and flipped the phone shut.

Mike got over Bill's stunt. He always did. It just meant the next few weeks would be stressful, since they'd already been totally strapped for cash. Even with the word spreading, they were lucky to do a couple hundred bucks a day at the trailer. So of course, the pumpkins put them in the red to start out the next week.

Thankfully, Mike had maintained a few connections from his time working on Lake Austin, and he'd been able to secure catering gigs for the river boats every now and then, when extra cash was required to save their necks.

A couple more weeks went by, and still, they had over half of the pumpkin hoard left to sell.

"Good investment, huh?" Mike said to Bill, his voice thick with sarcasm. "Guess in addition to tacos, I need to start making pumpkin pies."

But Bill's Hail Mary ended up paying big dividends when—a week from Halloween—a news van came rattling up to the trailer just as Mike was locking up for the night.

"Can I help you guys?" Mike asked, as alarmed as he was confused.

"We're with News Eight Austin….do you know you're the only people with pumpkins in all of the city?" the anchor asked.

"You're kidding," Mike laughed.

"There's another guy all the way out in Lake Travis. But that's it. If you don't mind, we'd like to do a story on you."

"Well, sure," Mike said, unlocking the door, smiling ear to ear. "Can I make you guys some queso?"

Mike was hoping the publicity would lead to a bump in sales, but once the story featuring Torchy's Tacos and the "last pumpkins in Austin" was on television, the little trailer wasn't just busy—it was swamped.

People just kept coming, one by one, lightening the 44-pallet load of pumpkins. Many of them, smelling the smoke from Juan's grill, then strolled over for a taco. When they'd finally caught up with the orders, Mike buzzed around the lot, greeting the guests and passing around samples.

That day, Torchy's posted its best day ever in sales. Mike leaned back in the trailer later that night, surveying the ransacked interior, still somewhat in shock.

"We are out of everything," Juan said with a look of pride.

"Pretty freakin awesome, huh?" Mike smiled. "I'll get to the commissary early in the morning to make sure we're restocked for tomorrow."

They looked out at Bill who was laughing with the last customer lingering in the lot.

"He was right," Mike said. "Pumpkins paid for themselves and we got money in the bank."

"He had a good idea, no?" Juan smiled.

"Yeah, he did…but don't dare tell him I said so."

Mike got to the trailer at sunrise the next morning and was surprised to find out that sales had continued throughout the night.

"Morning, Monk," Mike said to the hobo sleeping on the picnic bench out front. "Want an egg taco?"

Monk rolled to his side and moaned. "No potatoes. Just bacon, chilis—"

"I know, I know," Mike said. "Potatoes tear your stomach up."

Mike went inside and made Monk's usual. He worked quickly, hoping to have a little extra time to prep in case their streak of pumpkin luck continued, and the trailer was, once again, busy as hell.

He plated up the steaming breakfast taco and carried it out to his buddy. Though Monk's presence wasn't a daily occurrence at the trailer park, he lived in the woods behind the creek and was somewhat of an unofficial security guard of those parts.

"Oh, here you go," Monk said. He caught Mike by the arm and slapped a wad of cash into his hand.

"What's this?" Mike asked.

"Last I counted—250 bucks. Sold some pumpkins for you last night."

"Well, I'll be damned," Mike said. It had been a good Halloween haul for this little devil after all.

PART TWO

CHAPTER 8

"Honey, It'll Be Just Like *Cheers*"

Word of mouth is king.

Austin, 2007. Farrell Kubena—after just one taco—decided he was in. Torchy's first outside business investment, like the fandom that would come years later, came by word of mouth.

Again, it started with Bill. Bill told Randy, his cement guy in the landscaping business, who told his friend Farrell, a builder in Austin, that he had to try the tacos from this little trailer on South First Street.

Randy did more than just suggest—he pestered Farrell for weeks. "They're the best tacos I've ever had. And he's got these cute little South American girls serving them up."

So, after a few weeks, Farrell decided to have lunch there, just to shut his friend up.

"Damn, these are good," Farrell said, shredded lettuce falling out of either side of his mouth. "I mean *really* good."

"Told you," a beaming Randy said to Farrell. "Best tacos in town."

Farrell peered into the shiny aluminum vessel where Mike was sweating over the hot grill. "Will you introduce me to the chef?"

Mike stepped out, a signature towel hooked over his neck and a smile on his face. After they talked for a minute, Farrell rubbed his full belly and cut to the chase. "This food is legit. Have you ever thought about opening up a restaurant? I mean a *real* restaurant?"

"Man, I think about it every day. This is a hard business. I've put everything I've got into it, and I still don't know if I'm going to make it," Mike said with an embarrassed laugh.

"Well, if you can create this kind of popularity without a building—or even air conditioning—no telling what you can do with a proper storefront." Farrell pointed to the line of sweaty patrons. "There's a reason this crowd is standing in this heat."

That day, like most days, the cars in the parking lot were as diverse as the guests themselves. You had the minivans with soccer moms, the suits in their BMWs, the college kids pedaling up on bikes. There might have only been picnic tables, but at the Torchy's tables, there was a seat for everyone.

"Take this, just in case." Farrell extended his business card.

"You're in construction?" Mike said.

Farrell was a serial businessman. Like Mike, he was an Austin transplant who'd stumbled into town and was never leaving. Since moving to Austin right out of high school, he'd done everything from custom glass to spec homes. Even though Farrell had already lost his shirt a time or two, he knew when something was a hit. And Torchy's was a hit. He wasn't thinking of a restaurant empire, of course, just the perfect little hole-in-the-wall.

"Thanks for trying us out," Mike said to Farrell, his demeanor easy, and his gratitude for any new customer apparent. He high-fived Randy. "Come back soon, dude."

ODESSA, TEXAS, 1979. ODESSA, like much of far West Texas, has always been known for two things: football and refineries. The culture is a mix of oil-rich and working class, and there in the middle of it, an angry, fatherless teen slumped on the front porch of his ranch house, waiting for his ride.

The bitterness, down in his bones, was apparent on his baby face, but his eyes lit up as a gleaming hot rod pulled up, his friend in the driver's seat. "Come on, Farrell! We're late!" the kid called.

The boy bounded down the front steps, hopped in shotgun, and the two drove off to football practice.

"I'm so sick of this," the boy told his mother later that night. He was talking about the hot rod, but what he meant was everything else—the clothes, the food, the shabby house they lived in. All of it, right down to the Hamburger Helper he knew his mother would be serving for dinner. "Why can't we ever have *anything*?" he asked, teeth clenched.

His mother was tired, but still holding on to her patience. She strolled over and bent down in her son's face.

"You can," she said, eyes blazing. "Farrell Kubena, you can have anything you damn well please. You just have to go out and get it."

The boy thought about those words all night, and the next day, he did something unthinkable—he quit the football team. He wasn't a star, but he was a solid backup. It was no small decision for a boy his age, particularly considering he was in Texas, where high school football was—and still is—a way of life and a way out of town. And in Odessa, for a kid like him, it was one of the few ladders thrown down into the pit.

But at 15, he'd made up his mind. He was done playing a boy's game. It was time to do a man's work.

WHAT FOLLOWED FOR FARRELL Kubena was a couple decades of a rollercoaster ride as an entrepreneur and businessman. He started working before he could drive, and his motto with any job he took on was simply this: "I can do whatever you can teach me."

That attitude served him well, and by the time he graduated high school, he was making a pretty decent living for himself as an instrument technician for compressor plants and refineries around West Texas. But he was always looking for the next thing.

For years he liked to indulge in a little risk, and investing in side projects almost served to scratch an itch. *Invest a little in a taco trailer in Texas that is barely staying afloat? Sounds like fun. It's just money. Let's take our chances.*

MIKE COULDN'T TELL YOU what made him do it. He'd heard good things about the guy, but if he was honest, he was operating on gut. Time would show that Farrell and Mike had a lot in common. Both men were raised by strong mothers in the absence of a father. Both had experienced some serious low points personally and professionally. Both were self-taught and were determined to figure things out on their own. Whatever it was—fate or chemistry or just plain luck—a few days after their meeting at the trailer park, Mike called Farrell up.

"I talked with my partner Bill about your offer, and we'd like to take you up on it," Mike said.

"Awesome!" Farrell shouted over the beeping machinery in the background. He was clearly on site somewhere. "Let's get together and start discussing how this would work."

Though Mike (and Torchy's) were the ones who stood to gain the most from the phone call, Farrell was buzzing when he hung up. Once again, he'd done what he does best. He'd seen a good thing and almost secured it.

Once the Torchy's team had secured its first real investors, its members made plans. Mike and Bill had already ordered a second trailer that they didn't really have the cash for, so Farrell and wife Rebecca fronted the money for it. They currently had the new trailer parked on West Sixth, a party district next to a bar called Little Woodrow's.

As their presence grew within the city, so did the local fandom. All along, Mike kept his hand in Austin's local hot sauce competition scene, so the Little Devil continued to receive accolades outside of the trailer park parking lot.

But still, it was day-to-day. Even without the help of his wife's shrewd accounting skills, Farrell saw some problems right away. "Mike, you guys are hemorrhaging money," he said early on.

Mike knew he was right. Despite the popularity, balancing the books felt like the proverbial rolling a rock uphill. While he was busting his tail on the culinary side of things, Bill was left at the helm to make some important financial decisions. And since Bill's landscaping business was taking up much of his time, Torchy's accounts didn't always get the scrutiny they deserved. Bill was creative, an idea guy with a penchant for risky spending, so Farrell felt the freedom to make some suggestions. Observations, really.

"You can't landscape the trailer park when you haven't paid for the produce yet," he said with a laugh.

Again, Mike knew his new partner could be right. Their landlord at the Austin Trailer Park and Eatery had already raised their rent in the short amount of time that they'd been there. It was the same everywhere. No one would do more than a year's lease for a trailer, and when and if they saw anyone doing decent business, they'd jack the rent up the next year.

Since the summer after he finished culinary (when he chilled on his mother's couch), Mike had dreamed of a "real" restaurant. But the start-up costs were always too high, and the lease requirements on buildings were too long—it was always more than he was ready to undertake.

"What if your landlord decides he's going to develop that land, or he makes you go month-to-month and then kicks you out because you've left trash on the ground? You're out of business!" Farrell pressed his argument. "And your menu is almost entirely scratch-made—you need space! Aren't you tired of hauling shit you've cooked back and forth to the restaurant?"

"Yeah, yeah," Mike said. "You don't have to keep going. I'm convinced. But we don't have the money."

"Then I'll raise it. I'll do whatever we've gotta do, but Torchy's won't survive without a more permanent home."

IF THERE WAS ONE common denominator shared by these four early owners, it wasn't money or experience or even talent—it was resourcefulness. Though they came from different backgrounds—building, sales, culinary, landscape design—they all had the unique ability to think on their feet, to problem-solve off the cuff. Mike aside, the others had fallen into the restaurant business and what they did not know, they quickly taught themselves. In short, they were scrappy.

But as Farrell and Rebecca began to take up more of the business load, Bill started to realize that his time at the little taco shop had a lifespan. He'd done his part; he'd been on the literal ground floor, but it was clear (particularly after the entrance of the Kubenas) that Bill's more laid-back approach would eventually cause a rift. His imprint had been on the genesis of Torchy's, but now that the business was up and running, it was clear that he and Farrell were going to continue to butt heads on how money—no matter how small the sum—should be spent.

Thankfully, everyone cared enough about Mike (and their little taco baby) to sort things out before there were any hard feelings. So, as graciously as possible, Mike switched his partnership from his old friend Bill to his new acquaintances, Farrell and Rebecca. The only hurdle that remained was finding a person who'd buy Bill out.

The restaurant was doing fine, but it wasn't killing it. Farrell and Rebecca had already sunk as much money as they felt comfortable into their little "watering hole," especially since it looked like it could be years (if ever) before they got a dollar of it back. The person to join the team couldn't just be your average restaurateur looking for an easy ROI. It had to be someone who was also scrappy. Someone who was okay with a decent amount of risk.

Then, Rebecca had an idea. An old associate of hers from California had just sold a couple of houses and moved to Austin with his nest egg.

"His name is Bob Gentry. Our work together wasn't in the restaurant industry, but I know he's good with customer service. He's good with people…and he's got money to invest," Rebecca said with a shrug of her shoulders.

So, the team extended an invitation, and Bob arranged to meet the gang and see Torchy's for himself.

Bob was friendly and talkative. Slightly older than the rest of the bunch and seemingly more worldly wise, he naturally gravitated to the role of unofficial spokesperson for Torchy's.

"Well, it's a trailer," Bob said, "but it's doing gangbuster business." He nodded at the growing crowd. Never in his life had he seen so many people standing in the 100-degree heat. They weren't waiting to win a vacation or to get a discount on a TV—they were just buying tacos.

But after he'd tasted the food, he knew why. It was a no-brainer. "I'm in."

The buy-out itself wasn't much, essentially a third of the company at the time. That's all it took. Bill was happy, Mike was happy, Bob was excited about his new project, and the Kubenas, strength renewed by their unified front, continued to dream of expanding.

One afternoon, while working on some modern duplexes in downtown Austin, Farrell was up on the rooftop and noticed a little Mexican restaurant had shut down. There was a woman in the parking lot, showing someone around.

"I guess that restaurant building is for lease now," Farrell said.

The roofer he was talking to was confused, but he obliged Farrell with a nod, still waiting for instructions on the apartments they were building.

"I gotta go now." Farrell smiled. He ran across the street, cutting in front of a car along the way. He might have been a bit zealous, but this tiny store might be just what Torchy's was waiting for. Their golden ticket.

"Hey, ma'am," Farrell called to the woman across the four-space parking lot. "Are you in charge of this property, by chance?"

THE DEVIL IS IN THE DETAILS

"I own it. I inherited it from my father. El Nopalitas went out of business recently, so we are looking for a new tenant."

"That's a shame," Farrell said. And to a certain extent, he actually meant it. He'd taken Rebecca out to eat there while they were dating. The place was tiny and run-down as hell, but it had character. "Well, I'm with Torchy's Tacos. You might have seen us. We've got this little trailer down the street," Farrell said, pointing in the direction of South First. "Anyway, if this building is available, we'd love to lease this from you."

The lady looked over at her current prospect and gave a nervous laugh. "Why don't you let me finish up with this gentleman. Give me 45 minutes?"

"Done."

Exactly 45 minutes later, Farrell came back, as asked, and put on his best Farrell charm.

After a couple hours, he rushed home to tell Rebecca: it was official. Torchy's finally had a real home.

"And the best part, it's only $2,200 a month," Farrell said.

"What's the square footage?" Rebecca asked. She was smiling, but her tone was as wary as ever.

"1,200…and I can see the wheels turning in that analytical head of yours. It's not big."

"Understatement of the century. Is having two restaurants within a mile of each other a good thing?"

"Don't know," Farrell said. "But I think so. It could solidify the presence we've already built on this street. You know, in case the rent gets too high, and we have to shut the trailer down." He paused. "You think I'm digging us a hole?"

"Not sure yet. But if so, hand me a shovel."

"What do you think?" Farrell asked Mike as they stood in the center of the little restaurant on El Paso Street.

"Damn thing is held together with duct tape and bailing wire," Mike laughed. "I mean, the foundation has shifted so much, you have to tape the walk-in cooler to the wall."

"Yeah, she's a bit worn."

Mike stared at the site, silently taking it all in.

"What are you thinking there, buddy?" Farrell asked, unsure if his partner was having run-of the-mill jitters or full-blown regret.

"Can we afford it?" Mike asked.

"I think so. If we buy our kitchen equipment used and paint it ourselves. You know, slap some lipstick on her. Get her Torchified."

"Is this the right move?" Mike said. "It feels big."

"It's not even 1,500 square feet," Farrell joked. But he knew what Mike meant. "Look, everything is big at first. Every decision you make in life carries some weight."

Mike nodded. "You're right. I actually remember when this used to be the Old Virginia Cafe. Lots of Austin history here. We can work with this." Mike looked around the empty building. The window unit rattled, water pooling onto the floor. "At the end of the day, it's not life or death—it's tacos."

WITH TWO TRAILERS AND the move into an honest-to-goodness building well underway, Mike was going to need help with operations, so once again, he reached out to a former comrade in arms from his Chuy's days—his old buddy Jay Wald.

Jay had already turned down Mike's offers a few times, but Mike knew in his gut the partnership was the right one. Jay had the right blend of ambition and work ethic. And frankly, the two of them just got along.

"I'm brick-and-mortar now," Mike told Jay, giving his friend yet another sales pitch. "I've got investors. I'm not saying everything is perfect, but the taco rocket has launched, man."

Then Mike brought in the big guns. Bob and the Kubenas had offered to give up a little of their percentages for the right person, and they trusted Mike that Jay was it. "I want to make you a partner," Mike said. "I know your value, and I want you around for the long haul."

Before Mike had finished his spiel, Jay was already ready to cave. Just like everyone else in the Austin restaurant world, he'd been hearing about Mike's little taco trailer. The one that was changing the scene. Torchy's food—and its culture—was pervasive. And cool.

"So, we're finally actually doing this thing?" Jay laughed in slight disbelief. "I'll be ready to start tomorrow."

CHAPTER 9

The Hungry Years

Entrepreneurs who want personal time should get a day job—now.

Austin, 2008. The morning of the opening on El Paso Street, Farrell was nervous. A trailer was one thing, but a real brick-and-mortar restaurant—that was the big leagues. It had been his personal crusade, but suddenly, that morning, he thought he might be sick.

To make matters worse, his new in-laws (with a solid 20-year background in catering) just happened to be in town. *Great,* Farrell thought, *they'll have front seats to watch this whole thing go down.*

"Excited to see what you're working on." Farrell's father-in-law clapped him on the back. Farrell knew the jury was still out on what his new in-laws thought of him, and about his work.

"You'll love it," Farrell said confidently and grabbed his coat. He led the group the couple of blocks over to El Paso Street, silently cursing himself the whole way.

The building was humble to say the least. Together, the four owners had scraped together $60,000 to get the place up and running. They'd called in favors from friends and a few of their earliest taco superfans. But even with Farrell's finishing touches, given the limited budget and the short timeframe, the little restaurant that only seated 25 people still felt like the dated Mexican café, right down to the old ice-block cement cooler in the back.

The group walked across the small parking lot, and Farrell hoped his in-laws didn't notice that of the four parking spaces, three of them were vacant just minutes before opening day. Being that it was wintertime in Austin, the French doors on the patio had been propped open, providing some cool, fresh air and a bit of ambiance. But otherwise, the place was a total dive.

Farrell held open the door for his family, and they entered the empty restaurant. You could hear a pin drop. Farrell nodded at Juan who peered out from the small kitchen through the pick-up window. It was Juan's nature to appear antsy, but even he looked especially nervous. They ordered, and though Farrell didn't have much appetite, he threw in a queso for the table. It didn't matter if it was breakfast time, he knew queso was putting their best foot forward.

His in-laws seemed pretty taken with the food, but Farrell could think of nothing but the lack of customers and sat quietly chewing while his wife made small talk.

Ding!

The bell above the door—the old one that came with the building—rang out.

Finally, Farrell thought. *A customer.* But he couldn't bring himself to turn around.

A couple minutes later, another *ding!*

Then another. And another. The door was singing, and the small restaurant was almost packed when Farrell finally gathered the courage to turn around. The line was queued up out the door!

"Anyone know where there's more street parking?" a guy called from outside. Farrell looked out the window at the cars illegally squeezed into the parking lot. The two runners on the floor were frantically trying to keep up.

"I gotta stay and help these guys," Farrell said just as his in-laws were scraping the last bit of queso from the bowl. He winked at Rebecca and then swooped around the room, emptying trash cans. He grabbed a pad from the bar and began taking orders from the guests in the line. The chorus of the singing doorbell was accompanied by the sound of order tickets sliding across the metal wire that stretched across the food window.

"Hey, Juan, let's turn some music on!" Farrell called happily. "Damn if we aren't going to make it."

WHEN JAY SHOWED UP to work his first day, he couldn't say for sure what he was expecting in the way of a commissary kitchen, but it sure wasn't a gas station with bars on the windows.

He stood coatless and shivering in the predawn January morning, pulling on the handle of a door that was clearly locked.

"Well," Jay looked at his new employee, the young cashier who'd joined him in the parking lot. "Know how to get in?"

"It's usually opened by now." She shrugged and yawned.

It was not even 6:00 AM yet, and Jay knew that in the service industry, he should just be pleased that anyone was willing to get out of bed this early, so he tried to remain calm.

"What do you do if it's not open?"

"Wait for Raul to get here," the girl said, as if he was dense.

"Raul?"

"He and his brother run the convenience store."

Jay swallowed his protest. This wouldn't be such a problem except that there was a little thing called a prep list. At most of the other restaurants he'd worked in, the service time was 11:00 AM. If he was still at Chuy's, he'd be in bed right now. It would be a couple more hours before he came in and enjoyed his morning coffee, maybe even listened to the radio while he calmly went down the checklist to prepare for the onslaught of customers.

But this was different. Torchy's also served breakfast, which was supposed to begin at 7:00 AM. And almost everything on the menu had to first be cooked in the makeshift commissary, then loaded into storage containers, and driven over to the two trailer locations. Dui, Torchy's second employee, would hop in the catering van Farrell had purchased, and, with any luck, the food would arrive still warm. The whole process had sounded a lot easier when Mike pitched it to him, but at that moment, it seemed like a grand joke. A scavenger hunt just to get the food ready to sell.

Jay waited patiently for the convenience store brothers to straggle across the parking lot and unlock the door, and then he began chopping onions as if his life depended on it. As he chopped, he performed a mental assessment, figuring out how to be the most efficient. *I'll start the meat first, then salsa.* In addition to having access to his workspace, he also needed to create a proper prep list.

Jay, like the core group he'd joined, had tenacity.

His first day might have been a shitstorm, but if he was honest, he could deal with the makeshift commissary. Once he had created a prep list, he implemented a few tricks, and soon, he was able to charge through it with a few minutes to spare. The bigger issue was space— there wasn't any. Not in the trailers, not in the commissary, not even in their new little brick and mortar. When the food trucks delivered shipments to the restaurant on El Paso, they would sometimes unload the boxes in the alleyway, because there was not a square inch of space on the tiny kitchen floor. Jay would unpack the 10-pound boxes of meat from the order, shoving them individually in Tetris-like fashion into the walk-in cooler.

Jay, like the rest of the team, realized he had to make up his own playbook. He would have to run the day-to-day operations without any kind of guide, relying on a simple combination of experience, trial and error, and good, old-fashioned busting his butt.

Mike hired Anna to work the register and serve as bookkeeper. She and Jay quickly learned to work together.

"Produce needs to get paid," she'd whisper, as the guys unloaded their dollies of veggies. "What should I do?"

Jay would scribble his signature on the check, wondering how long he had until they cashed it.

Anna also had a very unorthodox means of doing payroll. She'd travel around from the stores to the trailers, collecting money and making change out of the cash drawer in the trunk of her sedan. She kept her little operation mobile because bank deposits had to be made daily. On payday, it became her habit to issue the checks Friday after 3:00 PM. Even though she didn't technically work weekends, she'd go by the locations on Saturdays and Sundays, deposit the weekend cash, and hope that the balance would still be above zero once the paychecks cleared on Monday.

Even with those great lengths, sometimes they still came up short, which meant Anna's least favorite responsibility of all—calling to ask for more cash.

"Hey, do you guys have any room on one of your credit cards? We're $8,000 short for labor this week."

The staff was small and Torchy's popularity was ever-increasing. Still, payroll always seemed to come around faster than they could handle it. And every time, they somehow worked it out. Thankfully, the majority of the people that came to work for them were gracious and understood what it was to give as much as they'd take.

Like an up-and-down game of Monopoly, after the first location on El Paso Street, Torchy's was able to lease another modest little property. The location was on Guadalupe Street. And though it was only 900 square feet, the store ushered them into the much-coveted heart of the University of Texas campus. The Torchy's menu was not a hard sell to college kids. In fact, it was a mega hit. The 18-22 age bracket became a free and very effective form of marketing for the entire brand.

Even with its growing success, gaining employees was not always easy. Torchy's had come up in South Austin, right at the bullseye of the "Keep Austin Weird" scene, and they embraced that. Though its fanbase was growing every day, Torchy's was a little too eclectic to attract standard servers. For the most part, people who took jobs in hospitality were typically clean-cut. But for Mike (and everyone else), appearances truly didn't matter.

"We don't care what you look like," Mike said to the new front-of-house hires. "We just need to know if you can be nice to the guests—and work."

The result? Some damn good employees who happened to have crazy hair dye and piercings. One by one, the applicants came in, those with purple hair and nose rings, the kind of folks who, historically, would have been a little too emo for traditional food service. But these people could thrive in a culture that gloried in eccentricity. A place not afraid to name a taco "Dirty Sanchez," and then shoot it out of a cannon at an opening-party crowd.

The Island of Misfit Servers might have been born of necessity, but soon, it was just another part of the brand.

BY 2009, THE BUSINESS had been going for almost four years and, just as Rebecca had predicted, she and Farrell had yet to receive a dime back from their investment. And that was okay by them. Farrell still believed the gamble was a good one (albeit a long game).

The rest of the team, however, didn't quite have that luxury. When there wasn't enough profit to go around, Mike and Bob had a simple way of figuring it out: "When is your mortgage due?" they'd ask each other.

The one whose mortgage came first got paid first.

Just like Mike had recognized he needed backup in the form of Jay, Jay realized he, too, needed more boots on the ground. So, the owners tried hiring managers for each location. It seemed like a good idea at the time. Every day, Torchy's was becoming more of a household name around Austin. More hands on deck would mean more food on tables and, eventually, more money in the bank.

But they hired managers too soon. It was one of their first learning experiences, thankfully, not one that cost them the business. The managers had no formal training, so their performances were subpar. And it might have been okay to carry them for a while, except there was barely enough cash to pay them in the first place. There was no reserve for dead weight. It was a perfect storm, and the owners weren't sure how to fix it.

But they didn't have long to think about it. In late 2009, Torchy's hit its first real financial crunch.

"Maybe we didn't do enough orientation. These managers needed more training protocol before we brought them on," Jay said at their "boardroom meetings" at the Kubenas' kitchen table. The manager failure was not only a business lesson, but an eye-opening observation of humanity. Some people—maybe even most people—were not meant to be self-starters.

"Well, whatever the reason," Rebecca said, spelling it out for them, "it's not working. And if we don't lighten the payroll load, we're going belly-up. In addition to the individual responsibilities we have for the company as a whole, it looks like a few of us need to go back in and act as managers for each of the locations."

The room fell silent. Another fork in the road. When you're already at 100 hours a week, more work is not just daunting, it's soul-crushing.

They looked around the table. They all knew if someone was wavering, now was the time to speak up, but instead, each of them gave an affirming nod.

"Jay will take El Paso," Mike said, "Bob has the trailers. Rebecca remains the de facto chair of finance, Farrell has maintenance and business development. I've got Guadalupe, and I guess, if I lose my house, I could just move in."

ALREADY EVERYONE HAD BEEN working overtime for as long as they could remember. The physical work was one thing—the heat of the trailer, the loading and unloading of the food from the commissary, hauling away trash and waste from the trailer park—but the emotional weight of making sure that those who were working for you were being taken care of was especially heavy. Still, they stuck together, hosting "board meetings" at the Kubenas' kitchen table on Wilson Street. They found themselves teetering on the edge of shutting the whole thing down and then, an unexpected catering order would come in, acting as a defibrillator.

Still, they dreamed of more. Optimism not only motivates; it helps pass the time. The Torchy's location on West Sixth was all electric and, seeing as how they needed a chargrill to parboil meats, they had to get creative. Mike and Jay rigged a propane tank behind the building and spent many early mornings grilling at 2:00 AM, after the bars closed.

"Dude, we are gonna get busted for this," Jay would say, as the smoke billowed down the alley.

On one of those nights, it was raining, so the two men huddled up under the old, torn canopy that came off the back door. They stood shoulder to shoulder, the meat hissed on the grill as they pulled their phones out, calculating. "If we had ten stores…and each of them could make $10,000 in profit a month…split four ways between all of us… that's $20,000 a month, per owner."

It was the ultimate dream. Too good to dare imagine.

Mike didn't even seem to notice that the rain poured down his shoulder from a hole in the canopy. "We'd be rocking and rolling, baby," he said.

IT TOOK ALMOST A year, but with the owners back in management roles, they righted the ship, and soon, Torchy's was financially stable enough to bring on new hires again. As Jay thought back through his Chuy's connections, one name came to mind: Alfonso Angelone, or "Fonz," as everyone called him.

And, as fate would have it, Fonz was newly unemployed and living two streets over from El Paso.

Fonz had heard through the restaurant grapevine about "Mike's new taco joint," but he didn't really know what to expect when Jay walked him back into the little El Paso kitchen.

"Fonz, I know you know how to run a restaurant—we've both been doing it for a decade—so this isn't a job interview," Jay said, "but I want to paint you the ugliest picture possible, so you know what you're getting into."

Fonz laughed, noting the humble surroundings.

"It's a modest operation, but people freakin' love this place," Jay said. "The food is crazy good. You won't have complaints."

Fonz thought it over. There was virtually no prep space, and the walk-in cooler was not much bigger than a port-a-let.

"I'm hiring you as GM, but you know what that means: you'll be food-running and cashiering...basically everything. One problem. You're actually taller than the people I've been looking to hire."

"There's a height requirement?" Fonz laughed.

Jay pointed to the vent hood just above the grill.

"Yeah, that's low," Fonz said.

"And you know you're going to be back here frying chips when we're slammed."

"Naturally."

"Oh, and there's no office space. Any questions?" Jay asked.

As it had happened many times before in Torchy's short history, and would happen again in the future, what should have been a tough sell, simply wasn't.

"You're right," Fonz said. "The food *is* damn good. See you tomorrow. 6:00 AM."

CHAPTER 10

The Gospel Spreads

Business doesn't break for life. And vice versa.

Trailer Park and Eatery, 2007. Even before the brick and mortars, when there was just the trailer and the dream of something big, Mike was used to sacrifice. His house was mortgaged. His hobbies were nonexistent. His social life was entirely made up of friends from AA meetings and the Torchy's crew. He did have a girlfriend, but with his workload, it was challenging to find time to grab dinner unless it was in his own restaurant.

He was definitely clocking more hours than ever before, but given his background in the food industry, he was already a seasoned veteran of overtime.

For years, he'd been busting his butt in a kitchen, but he had to admit, using creative passion to make his own food meant carrying the workload differently. He didn't want to stop. He prayed for more daylight. He simply needed his body to hold out long enough to get him through the 16-hour days. Most days, the work was less grind and more joy.

When he watched people's faces as they tasted the food. When he overheard his own name around Austin. When he read reviews with words like "innovative" and "inspired," and of course, "damn good," it was all worth it.

Even so, some early mornings, before the city was awake and the riverboats were running, he'd drive his Vespa by Lake Austin. The sky was just barely orange with the sunrise, and he'd see the misty, cool surface of the lake and dream about a day on the water. *No work. Just for one day.* But at that point, with all his responsibilities, even one day away was impossible. The local lake might as well have been 1,000 miles away.

His mother called every now and then from D.C. to check in. He knew she'd been bragging to all her friends. "He's making world-class cuisine in a trailer down in Texas."

Mike had learned hard work, in part, from his mother. While he was growing up, more often than not, Karen had two jobs—the newspaper and somewhere else.

"I'm sorry I've been so busy, mom," he said when they were on the phone one night.

"Don't be. You're building your career. It takes all your time and energy to establish yourself."

"Definitely feels like it."

"Look, I don't want to be in your way," his mother said, "but I'm thinking I'll come down to see you. I've got to try one of these tacos for myself."

It was a mild afternoon. Karen Timmons sat under a tree and read a book while her son made tacos. He'd planned their late lunch for a weekday around 4:00 PM, so he wouldn't be totally slammed at the trailer, and they could enjoy each other's company.

"Order up," he said, sliding the food across the picnic table.

"What have we got?" she asked excitedly.

"This one," Mike said pointing to one of his signature tacos, "is the Trailer Park. It's a crowd favorite—fried chicken, green chilies, lettuce, pico, cheese, and creamy poblano ranch…and I made it 'trashy,' which means I put queso on top."

When it was time to go back to the airport, she was still talking about the queso. "You keep getting better and better," she said, hugging him tightly.

"I've missed you, Momma."

"This is amazing." She looked around. "I'm so proud of you."

"Well, we'll see. We're in a trailer for gosh sakes, but the word is getting out. Thank you for all you've done to get me here."

It was only a few months after her trip that Karen called her son again. This time, it was to tell him the news: *cancer.*

"There are a few complications, but my prognosis is good," she said cheerfully.

"Mom, tell me what you need, and I'll do it. I can take time off. Come up there for a few days or something."

"No, no, I'm fine. The doctors are taking good care of me here. You keep focusing on your business," she insisted.

Mike wouldn't find out until a month before her death that the optimistic updates his mother had been giving him over the phone amounted to a bunch of bullshit. But that was her way. Take the hard road alone. It was also her final attempt to protect him.

But the real truth was just one of the hard facts of life. She was very sick. Nine months after her fight began, she was gone.

Just as he'd done when he came to the restaurant business in the first place, Mike threw himself into his work, using it to escape his grief. The first time, he was grieving the loss of a lifestyle, the loss of the drugs that, as a lost teenager, he'd built his life on. This time, it was more than that. He was grieving the person who had been the sole member of his family for so long—his best friend.

So after she was gone, he made a promise. He would work harder, trusting that somewhere, somehow, she was watching him and just hoping to God he was still making her proud.

The cycle of joy and grief would happen again and again. Torchy's whirlwind of growth—the Little Devil's milestones—occurring right alongside his own personal seasons. Celebration, sadness, and celebration again.

Mike got married. The courtship happened in a cloud of activity—the explosion of his young company and the loss of his mother. Then, ten months after the honeymoon, Mike became a father. His son, Mike Jr., would be the great gift out of a marriage that would be short-lived.

As a new father, Mike's purpose shifted yet again. He didn't just want Torchy's to succeed for himself and his Torchy's partners. He wanted it for the tiny, wide-eyed boy who was counting on him.

OVERALL, ALL FIVE OF the owners shared a desire to use Torchy's as a second chance for many of those they might hire. They were okay with it, even if it bit them in the ass. It was also understood that Mike's heart wasn't going to change, so even Bob began to embrace it.

Personal relationships was one area Bob had always excelled in. Since he was fluent in Spanish, Bob had a special bond with some of the staff, the ones whose English was enough to get around the kitchen but not much more. They had a nickname for him—*viejito*—little old man.

Bob was also the informal Torchy's greeter, walking around the trailer park parking lot, shaking hands and talking to customers, asking how they liked the food, where they were from. He was doing this very thing one afternoon, and that's when he noticed a competitor was scoping them out.

It was a group of six or seven people, dressed nicer than the average customer. In Austin, locals usually dressed casually, so these guys, with their collared shirts and similar dress, immediately stood out. They sat at a picnic table, sampling every taco on the menu with multiple baskets of chips and salsa and queso. Bob, unable to stand his curiosity, wandered over and engaged in small talk and discovered they were a traveling research group with Kentucky Fried Chicken. Their objective: to figure out a good handheld food item for the KFC menu. Something that had a walkable element to it, as opposed to fried chicken on a plate.

"How about that?" Mike said when Bob told him. "Scoped out by Colonel Sanders."

The press, the notoriety, the attention the little taco underdog was getting shouldn't have been a surprise. The food was good—and people had figured that out. Never mind that behind the curtain, the Torchy's team was just scrambling to seem like a legit company, and with each week that passed, there was a new problem to figure out.

Though they were still somewhat finding their way, they swung for the fence. "It takes some balls to grow a company," as Farrell had said.

No better example of this was in 2009, when they decided to take the plunge and participate in Austin City Limits. The weekend-long music festival in Austin's Zilker Park seemed like the perfect place to showcase the Little Devil. Torchy's was a local standout—and they had six locations at this point—but joining the festival would be a huge investment of time, energy, and resources. For starters, to be a food vendor, you had to pay $35,000 upfront for a single booth. The price tag was significant, but Mike thought it was worth the risk. He stood by his old adage: *If I can just get the food into people's mouths, they'll come back.*

"Sooo, where do you suggest we start?" Jay stood with Mike, staring at the prep lists lined up on the chrome countertop.

"Well," Mike said. "I've fed the masses before, but 70,000 is definitely going to be a new record. We need to rent a refrigerator truck."

The preparation took weeks. They hired more staff. With the additional 20 people working around the clock, Jay and Mike figured there was a chance they'd be ready for ACL. That is, if everyone put in overtime.

They made salsa in ten-gallon buckets and then schlepped those buckets to and from locations. One of them actually tipped over in Bob's car, covering his backseat in freshly diced tomatoes.

Bob wasn't alone in sacrificing his vehicle on the altar of prep.

"Something is wrong with my truck, man," Dui complained to Jay as they unloaded yet another case of to-go boxes. "I mean, I've cleaned it and everything...it still stinks. *Really* stinks."

Jay shrugged it off, but after a few days of Dui's complaints, Jay went out to see for himself.

"That is rank, dude!" Jay said, pulling his shirt collar over his nose. "It's the wheel well. What did you spill in there?"

"Eggs." Dui shrugged. "Two weeks ago."

With that, Jay marched inside to the cash register and pulled out $200. "Get a detail on us."

As it turned out, the sacrifice, at every level, was worth it. A couple of hours into the festival, the energy, the sales, the long lines at the booth made it clear: the ACL gamble had paid off.

"I only wish we'd had 50K to get the double booth instead of the single," Jay said to Mike as they walked out to their cars, dog-tired and deliriously pleased with the day's success. Dressed in the bold red and black Torchy's T-shirts, they looked something like a rock band. They walked quickly, each clutching the straps of their backpacks while trying to act nonchalant. Back in those days, Austin City Limits dealt mostly in cash, which meant vendors were carrying around thousands and thousands of dollars in loose bills. They needed to get the backpacks emptied into a safe at the Kubenas' house on Wilson Avenue.

"This shit is like *Ocean's Eleven*, dude," Jay whispered to Mike.

"Tell me about it," Mike laughed. "Never been so nervous in my life."

They'd almost made it across the long parking lot to their cars when someone called out, "Hey!"

Mike didn't look up, but instead, the two just walked faster.

"Hey!" the guy called again. "Are you guys with Torchy's?"

Jay and Mike looked at each other cautiously, then nodded.

"Well, hell yeah!" the guy shouted. "We love Torchy's!"

"Thanks for the support, man." Mike smiled, a little confused by his first encounter with true fandom.

"Torchy's! Torchy's! Torchy's!" the guy began chanting. A few friends that were with him joined in.

Jay waved to the group as he ducked into Mike's car. They'd been so worried about getting robbed, but instead, they were cheered.

Mike turned to Jay. "That was weird and cool. Think they were wasted?"

"Actually…" Jay said, "I don't. I think they are just true fans."

Rebecca was waiting at her 10-foot kitchen table for the boys to get back. "How did it go?" she asked. "Was it crazy?"

"See for yourself." Mike unzipped his backpack, and cash spilled out onto the table.

Rebecca's jaw dropped.

Jay dumped out his backpack and added to the money pile, bills littering the kitchen floor.

"Shut the blinds!" Rebecca said. "We look like we're money laundering!"

"We made some money today," Jay said. "Has to be at least 40 grand."

"But that's not all," Mike said. "Jay, tell him what happened. People were actually cheering for us when we left. This thing is catching on, man."

The ACL event was a milestone. A moment in time where the team had said to themselves, "We might do great, we might do terrible, but the opportunity is here. We have to try."

They went into the festival with a chip on their shoulder: No, they weren't the traditional Mexican restaurant. That was the point.

Years later, the owners would mark this event as the start of the phenomenon that would become the Little Devil's cult following.

The gospel was beginning to spread.

CHAPTER 11

"You Ain't Seen Jesus Yet"

Risk everything. Then do it again. There's no cashing in.

Austin, 2009. The long game was starting to feel like perpetual hand to mouth. Mike was trying to be patient, but the fact was, he'd been busting his ass to make ends meet ever since he was seventeen. He took his first job—delivering newspapers in the neighborhood—right after he'd turned eight years old. His whole life had been work, work, work—and wait for any kind of compensation.

"Dude, the company's making money," he'd say to Farrell every now and then. "I want to finally have some money. Nothing crazy, I just want to be comfortable. Not strapped every month."

But for five or six years, Farrell's advice had always been the same: "Be patient, man. If we keep using profits to open new restaurants, we've got new sources of revenue, and that revenue is only going to build over time."

"You said that a year ago."

"I know. And it's true today. I promise—the money train is going to hit us in the ass, we just have to be patient. It'll be worth the wait."

"I trust you, man," Mike conceded. "Just hope I live long enough to see some fruits of our labor," he added with a laugh.

Mike wasn't the only one feeling the exhaustion of work without monetary reward, but each of the owners homed in on what they could bring to the table to keep Torchy's not just going but growing.

As Jay saw it, one of the first big hurdles was the point-of-sale system, or POS. Shortly after the store opened in El Paso, it was clear that writing order tickets by hand and clipping them on a wire was not going to work for the long haul. They needed to itemize, systemize, and digitize so that things would be fluid from store to store, and all of these "izes" would require a legitimate computer system to keep tabs on sales and inventory.

So again, like he did with the prep lists, Jay set to work figuring it out. Once they had the point-of-sale system established, the box cars were all hooked to the train, so to speak, and this cohesion allowed them to graduate to more operations.

Farrell, for his part, continued looking for spaces where Torchy's could grow. With a little guidance from friends in real estate and a lot of instinct, he acquired a handful of brick-and-mortar locations by taking over leases of smaller restaurants and eateries. One of them had been on Guadalupe Street. Though it was the smallest building—the restaurant wasn't even 1,000 square feet—since it was smack in the university district, it paid some big dividends with UT college kids.

Since the start, every space they'd leased had been a hit, and so Farrell was forever driving around Austin in his white Chevy, dreaming of expansions. Bob and Rebecca had been reporting the numbers, and the profits were good. Really good. By 2010, the trailer was seeing some $5,000 to $6,000 days on a weekend. In Farrell's mind, the increasing profits confirmed that it was time for the next leap, so when he saw an opening for lease at Arbor Trails, the shopping center in southwest Austin, he threw their hat in the ring.

Arbor Trails was nothing like the little spaces they'd assumed before. It was a power center, a place for established chains. A quirky underdog like Torchy's was not a likely candidate, but Farrell liked the location's visibility. There also weren't great restaurants in the center at the time, so he figured it was worth sending a letter of intent. Just for the hell of it.

A few days later, Farrell got a call. It was Gray Stogner, a well-known name in Texas real estate.

"Personally, I don't think you're ready to put in a store in a property like this one," Stogner said. "But the building is yours…if you want it."

Farrell was stunned. It was one of the few times that he didn't know what to say. "Thank you," he coughed, trying to cover up both shock and excitement.

"You should know that the lease term is seven and a half years," Stogner added cautiously.

"We're prepared for that. We plan on a long, successful partnership. Mr. Stogner, I'm sure you had offers from companies far more established than ours. If I may be so bold…why'd you choose us?"

Stogner paused. "Well, honestly, I'm doing it for my daughter."

"Your daughter?"

"Her name is Darby. She goes to UT. She took me to eat at your little restaurant near campus. When I told her you guys wanted my space at Arbor Trails, she freaked out. She said I had to give it to you. Torchy's is her favorite restaurant in town."

"Well, what'd you think of it?"

"Food was good. And the place was packed. Anyway, she insists you guys are a winner, so I promised her I'd give you a chance."

"Thank you, sir," Farrell said. "You won't be disappointed."

Once they had a signed lease to the Arbor Trails building, there was just the small problem of outfitting it so that it was a proper restaurant. Kitchen equipment, supplies, décor, a few repairs—to ready a store like that one would cost a small fortune. Even though Torchy's had been approved for the lease, with their current financial situation, no bank was going to give them a line of credit for set-up costs.

This was no surprise.

They'd been through this already with the smaller locations, but in Torchy's-fashion, they'd found a scrappy way around it. Working together, they'd secured personal loans to fund their new stores. In return for the investment, the private investor got double-digit percentages—somewhere around 25 percent—of that individual store's sales for three to five years.

But Arbor Trails was going to be their biggest store yet. Even if they cut some corners and did everything themselves, they still needed at least $80,000 to get it open, and they weren't really sure where they were going to get it.

Then, an option presented itself within their own ranks. Fonz, after just four months as a Torchy's GM, was not only deeply committed to the company, he'd also realized it was a sure bet. He'd worked in various restaurants for fifteen years before Torchy's, so he knew a thing or two about what constituted a restaurant's success.

He explained it to his wife over dinner one night. "It doesn't even matter if the ticket times are running long, every time I take the food to the table, I can't go wrong."

With that confidence fueling him, Fonz enlisted himself (and his in-laws) as the investors for the new big box store at Arbor Trails. With Fonz and his family funding the endeavor, Torchy's would be able to get its newest (and potentially most lucrative) store up and running.

Since, as usual, they didn't have any money to hire a contractor, the team attempted to give the building a facelift. Unlike the other little hole-in-the-walls where Torchy's had taken up residence, Arbor Trails was a much newer building. That meant while they would still need their hammers, the prep in general would require a lot less duct tape.

As they saw it, the building was functional but it needed flair. Fonz's family funds had been enough to secure the necessities, but when it came down to décor, the money had to be stretched.

One thing that made Torchy's special was its emphasis on variety. When it came to food quality and the brand's vibe, Torchy's was very consistent, but with the menu (namely the Taco of the Month) and the actual storefronts, they wanted to keep it interesting. So each restaurant was different—from the table layout to the marquee. They wanted people to be surprised. It wasn't something that they'd necessarily spelled out in a company manifesto, but as Mike had said, "We can go be McDonald's and have the perfect little mold, or we can do something creative every time. Keep the locations as inspired as the food we're serving."

It was with that mindset that the group examined the bare restaurant at Arbor Trails. "I think we need something we can put across a whole wall," Farrell said. "Not like tile, but something that has some dimension, some depth."

Mike joined him, standing before the blank walls.

"What if we used fake flowers?" Farrell asked.

"Guess that could work." Mike cocked his head.

"We need something to secure the flowers to…something cheap… chicken wire!" Farrell said, smiling.

"Dude, you're surprising me more and more every day," Mike laughed.

"You just keep using your creativity in the kitchen," Farrell said. "We'll keep the creativity in the building."

After the other stores were closed for the night, Mike joined his partner in his most unorthodox construction project yet.

"Saved you a hot glue gun." Farrell nodded at one of the tables where supplies were scattered about. Since they all had day jobs, the decorating was exclusively an after-hours venture.

Jay came through the front door and found Mike and Farrell hand-rolling fabric into fake roses. "What the hell, guys?" he asked, part teasing, part genuine curiosity.

"We're making a sort of mural…and you can't just stick the flowers up here," Farrell said, not turning away from the wall. "You gotta pinch and hold it till the glue dries. That's part of what takes so long."

Jay watched, dumbfounded, as his coworkers hot glued their fingers to the wall.

"It's gonna look better with actual daylight coming through the windows," Farrell said. "These fluorescents don't do it justice."

Jay shook his head. "This is so far beyond blood, sweat, and tears…"

"Yeah, I actually think I don't have any fingerprints anymore," Farrell said.

"Okay," Jay said tentatively, "I've gotta get home cause I'm gonna get up early and start doing prep. You guys don't stay up too late."

"I like how it kinda plays tricks with your eyes," Mike said, staring back at the wall. "The dimension is nice. One question: Is the health department going to be okay with this?"

"Dammit, man!" Farrell burned another fingertip. "Don't ask me now that we're almost done! I don't care—we're keeping it until someone tells us to take it down."

Farrell was too tired to look at the time when he locked the glass front doors at Arbor Trails that next morning, but based on the predawn light, he guessed it was somewhere around 4:00 AM. The rest of Austin was still asleep. The parking lots around them were all empty. The sky was gray, the air cool, and the traffic on the interstate quiet. If he hurried, he could go home and take a quick shower before he came back to do the final preparations for the grand opening.

Even with weeks of working through the night, the store was still not going to be ready. When he came back an hour later, the small team of Torchy employees raced around like the mice before Cinderella's ball. Most of them were too busy to comment, but a few people noticed Farrell's floral wall mural. While a bit random for a taco shop, they all agreed it was totally impressive.

It was only a couple of hours before the doors were supposed to open, and Farrell's nerves were as bad as they had been the morning they opened up on El Paso Street. In fact, they were worse. If El Paso conjured up well-founded jitters, this was another feeling all together. It was straight-up fear.

But what he'd done with this—signing a near decade-long lease in a busy shopping center—was letting it all ride. And he wasn't just shoving his own chips out onto the table. It wasn't even that he was dragging Rebecca into it. It was Mike and everyone else as well. To make it even more intense, Mike and his wife had recently announced that they were expecting their first child. These were all the things Farrell thought about as the clock ticked down to opening time.

"Dude, let me help you with that," Mike said, reaching for the massive aluminum mobile that Farrell was attempting to hang from the ceiling. The mobile was crafted with an eighth-inch Plexiglas and aluminum flat panel and shaped like an enormous cloud. Their buddy Floyd, a local welder, had helped them design the statement piece. It was his idea to use aluminum, since it was cheap. "You get more for less," Floyd had said, but the problem was they'd made it almost too big. It was almost the length of the room but Farrell stood there on a ladder, trying to hang one side of it from the rafters with wire.

Mike took the other side, and in silence, the two men struggled with the mobile until it was secure.

"All right. What's next?" Mike looked over at his partner, but Farrell was off somewhere, in his own head.

"You okay, man?" Mike asked.

"No…don't think I am this time." Farrell stared catatonically through the glass doors. "We've taken risks before, but this one was too big."

"What are you talking about?"

Farrell walked over to the other side of the restaurant and pointed out the window. "The parking lot. It's freakin' empty!"

But Mike was cool, relaxed…smiling even. "Don't worry, brother. They haven't met Jesus yet."

125

"I'm being serious. We got *a lot* riding on this."

"I am too. Just let me get food into their mouths. Trust me—they'll be convinced."

Mike had always come in like an unexpected wind to the sail, bolstering morale when anyone started to waver. His quiet confidence—devoid of ego—was almost spiritual. He believed in what he was making and that he was supposed to keep making it, despite the obstacles. If he just kept trying, the rest would work itself out.

And it did. Just like the previous store openings, right before the doors were unlocked for the first time, the line of hungry taco lovers seemed to instantly materialize—and wrap around the block.

All told, in its first month in business, after all expenses were paid, the Arbor Trails location cleared $10,000. The team gathered again at the Kubena kitchen table and stared over Rebecca's shoulder at the numbers.

"That's $2,000 a piece...for each of us...from just one store!" Jay said, turning to Mike. "This was the dream, and we're doing it, man."

"Let's keep rockin' and rollin'," Mike laughed. "This is only the beginning."

CHAPTER 12

Leaving the Nest

Every new restaurant is like going through the birth canal again.

Austin, 2010. It had only been a few months since Arbor Trails was up and running when Farrell got a phone call.

"Farrell, it's Gray Stogner."

"Gray," Farrell said, slightly unnerved by the surprise call.

"Listen, I've got this building available, and it would be perfect for you guys," Stogner said.

"Okayyyy," Farrell said. "What part of Austin is it in?"

"It's not...It's in Dallas."

"Dallas? We can't come to Dallas. It's all we can do to manage what we've got going on here."

"Time to push you out of the nest," Stogner said with a laugh.

"You said yourself we weren't ready for Arbor Trails. And that was just a few months ago. We're finally seeing some decent profits. We have so much going on here, we don't want don't want to potentially sabotage—"

"I get it. It's risky, but you guys have already proven yourself. You need to look at this."

Farrell sighed.

"Trust me on this."

"Okay...tell me more."

The next day, Farrell took off for Dallas to check out the space. He knew he was close to the building, but even with the GPS, he couldn't find it.

He called up Mike. "Strike one, man. Stogner told me the building was on Forest Lane and Preston, but I need a damn treasure map...I've been driving around for ten minutes, and I don't see it."

"That's not good," Mike said.

"No kidding. It's definitely not visible from the road. Wait... wait...here we go. I haven't gone this way...it's behind the Potbelly's. Found it."

"So...it's not the location of the century, as Gray suggested?" Mike said.

"No."

"Well, why's he pushing it so hard?"

"Cause he's damn good at business. He has this space, and he wants it filled. He knows if he has the first Torchy's in Dallas, it's going to be successful." Farrell was guessing, but he was pretty sure he was right.

"What's your gut telling you?" Mike asked.

"My gut…" Farrell pulled into a space in front of the building and sat there, thinking for a minute. "I guess it's to gamble on him, like he did on us. See how it plays out. Plus, he said he'd give us the deal of the century."

"Okay, man," Mike said. "Unless you see something big and hairy inside that building that totally scares you off, I say let's do it. Let's go to Dallas."

Torchy's was in no way a "Big Bang" of success. Each added location was painful. The growth of the Little Devil was the result of months and years of dogged resilience. Fervent trial-and-error in the days before you could YouTube everything.

Moving Torchy's to another city would further complicate an already exhausting process. They'd been slowly moving across Austin, but going to Dallas was a Hail Mary from the 50-yard line. It was also upping the ante on an already high-stakes gamble. From a statistical standpoint alone, any restaurant chain that fell under the broad umbrella of Tex-Mex was known for not traveling well. Even if the move was as short (and as simple) as Houston to San Antonio, it invoked a little trepidation. Torchy's had been dubbed "intrinsically Austin," so the team had to wonder, *Would it take elsewhere?* Its quirky culture had bloomed in the petri dish of a city that understood (and valued) its irreverence. Would that translate in another city? They were local darlings, no doubt, but what about outside their hometown?

The Torchy's team started the Dallas transition by recruiting and hiring a local crew. Since it was 2010, they threw up a Craigslist ad for managers. From it, they got a long list of interested parties and ultimately, the first assistant managers for their "satellite" store—two mildly experienced, fresh-faced 20-somethings: Ben Talbot and Kate Haas.

Kate, newly graduated from college up in Chicago, had just been in Dallas only a day or two when she saw the ad. She had no real restaurant experience, but she read the description for the management position and thought: *This sounds like something I could do.*

She interviewed with Jay, and to her surprise and utter delight, he called her back before she'd even made it home. She hadn't even been in Texas for 24 hours, and already she'd landed a big girl job! Somehow, she managed to hit it out of the park on her first swing, and she wasn't going to mess it up.

Unlike Kate, Ben knew his way around the restaurant industry. Like Jay and Fonz, so far in his young life, he'd already racked up years of good and bad experiences in both the front and the back of the house. Admittedly, from a leadership standpoint, he had some room for growth, but he was knowledgeable and definitely not afraid of hard work.

Ben had been there, done that, and he was also over the corporate BS. When he saw the ad and scoped out Torchy's website, he knew instantly that this wasn't going to be the same old gig.

"Dirty Sanchez?" he laughed to himself as he scrolled down the menu. "These sound like my kind of people."

For Kate, the shock and excitement gave way to nerves when she arrived in the small kitchen and realized just what she'd signed up for.

Though Ben would be her co-manager, there was a staff of 30 or so to oversee, many of whom only spoke Spanish. There were also recipes to learn and countless processes to go over: payroll, delivery trucks, sanitation regulations. Her head was swimming.

Thankfully, what superseded all of the unknowns was the pervasive welcome that came from that same kitchen. It didn't matter what their role was, everyone who was there seemed genuinely happy to be there. Kate quickly realized what she might have lacked in restaurant experience (or even basic language skills), the smiles and the general body language more than made up for. The cliché of the warm family kitchen was playing out before her eyes.

The new hires were not the only ones adjusting. The owners were navigating some new terrain as well. The whole experience, on the one hand, was an exercise in letting go. It would be the first time their baby was outside their sight. Since they weren't going to be able to physically check in on the store every day, they did their best to instruct and guide from Austin. Again, they focused on their areas of expertise: Farrell secured the particulars of the building, Rebecca helped arrange the funding for the new location, and Bob—the de facto public relations chair—began the marketing efforts. As far as implementing both the recipes and the culture of Torchy's, Mike, Jay, and Fonz would be the ambassadors into the uncharted territory.

During the three-week training period in Austin, Mike was back in the kitchen, cooking and passing out samples to Ben and Kate and the rest of the new team. "Taste this," he said, offering them anything from a bite of crispy fried chicken to a hot tortilla chip. "This is what it should taste like. This exactly. No exceptions."

Ben whispered to Fonz, "Is he always this intense?"

"About the food? Yes. With everything else, he's laid back as hell, but if the food is not perfect, don't bother serving it!"

The training period was relatively short for restaurant managers and largely informal, but it was also intuitive, personal, and nuanced. There were no corporate strata to get through. Mike and Jay, in particular, burned up I-35 between Dallas and Austin, and when they couldn't be there in person, they made sure they were available. The owners didn't hand out training manuals (because they didn't have any printed just yet), but they did give out their cell phone numbers, with the instruction: "Call me any time."

For Jay, the transition was particularly challenging. Once again, he was laying track with a speeding train already whistling behind him. Since the decision to set up shop in Dallas was so sudden, the team didn't have time to create proper training protocols for each of the positions, but the Dallas store provided an opportunity for heavy self-reflection. In a sense, they'd done it backwards. They'd started with the product and then had to reverse engineer the instruction manual. Before they could share the core values, processes, and practices of Torchy's to out-of-town restaurants, the owners needed to be able to articulate them. This meant a lot of discussion among the partners. Many of the new hires had spent very little—if any—time inside a Torchy's.

"We had to be able to explain something we knew intrinsically," Jay said, "but at that point, we had to stop and define who we are. Every new store is like going through the birth canal again."

They kept coming back to two catchphrases: *The devil is in the details*—the freshest cilantro, the perfectly crispy chip, the queso placed on the table at just the right temperature—and *If it ain't damn good, don't serve it.*

Besides an undying commitment to food quality, there was another element that Jay and the rest of the founders hammered home: *Be honest with guests. Tell them the truth.*

"Get comfortable with this phrase: *We messed up. How can we make it right?*" Jay said to those who'd be on the floor. "Because there are going to be times when you'll have to use it."

As opening day approached, it wasn't just Farrell who wondered if their luck was bound to run out. The rest of the partners had the same fears. Along with the general buzz from superfans and Austin transplants, the *Dallas Morning News* also featured Torchy's, the new taco joint in town. Despite the publicity, the partners collectively held their breath, wondering if the masses would follow them yet again.

And they did. Well, they tried to.

Unlike the opening day experience at other locations, some of the fans who'd been waiting for Torchy's had trouble finding them. Since the building on Forest Lane couldn't be seen from the road, people were driving around, calling the store. "Hey, where are you guys?" they'd ask.

Ben and Kate got very good at giving directions. Oddly enough, in the early days, the young managers were almost thankful for the somewhat hidden location because it gave them a little time to catch their breath between guests.

There was also another phone call they got from time to time. "Are you guys on a long wait? We can see people lined up."

Of course, this was often true—there was a wait—but other times, it was an optical illusion. The confusion was an unanticipated result of yet another piece of Farrell's décor. Once again, he'd commissioned a buddy to do some custom work on the cheap. The result: a beautiful metal wall of people, which, if you saw it from the road, could be mistaken for a line out the door.

Once the store had opened, with each day that passed, the crowd seemed to grow like a snowball barreling down the slope. Customers had found the store, and they were hungry. A couple of weekends in, the Dallas location was unofficially the busiest a Torchy's had ever been. The owners had gone back to Austin by now, so the young managers, Kate and Ben, looked around their store, panicked. Ticket times were long, the line wrapped the building, and at that moment, the new team's kitchen was completely overwhelmed. It was sink or swim. They gave each other a quick pep talk. "We're gonna get through this. We just have to do what they taught us—go to the guests and tell them the truth."

And so they did. As people came in and ordered, the managers circled the room. "We're so glad you're here, but just so you know,"

Kate said, forcing a worried smile, "it may be 45 minutes to an hour before you get your food. Is there anything I can get you while you wait?"

She winced, bracing for some kind of complaint, the threat of a poor Yelp review, even an eye roll, but instead, the response she got left her totally dumbfounded.

"That's fine," the people in line said, smiling. "We're just happy that you guys are here in Dallas."

"Great!" she said. "I'll go ahead and get you guys something to drink."

The truth actually worked.

And then, some unexpected backup appeared. "Hey, guys," Fonz said as he maneuvered through the front door crowd and made his way back to Kate and Ben. "Either of you learned how to grill cook yet?"

Grill? They both shook their heads. Of course, they hadn't been grilling, they'd been running a store for heaven's sake.

"Well, you need to watch then." He threw on an apron and turned his ball cap backwards. And just like that, he slipped into the line without messing up anyone's rhythm, much like a girl on a playground jumps through the ropes of double dutch.

With Fonz's help, it wasn't 30 minutes before the long trail of white order tickets fluttering in the window had cleared and finally, they were out of the weeds.

"Here's the thing," Fonz told them after the last table had been cleared for the night and the register spit out its five-foot sales report.

"Nobody's gonna force you to go above and beyond. Most restaurant managers consider certain jobs beneath them. They're the types who stay in their lane…but those are the crappy managers. And not only are they not respected—they don't last. Know how to do everything your team does, so you can help when you can."

After another couple of weeks, the team felt like it was finally safe to say it out loud—Dallas, like its sister stores in Austin, was a huge success. And it had potential to be the biggest hit yet.

Again, it seemed to be the strange result of determination and luck. They chose the right people to manage the store, people who were willing to work, who were fiercely loyal, and who could problem-solve and grow in their weak spots. While it might have been good luck or divine intervention, it was the proverbial scratch-off card that came out a winner. But the owners also put in the work, the hours upon hours of personal investment to ensure that what was planted would bear fruit.

With the Dallas store proving to be a success, Torchy's was entering into a new era of sorts. No longer were they just cool in Austin. This thing had legs. And while they were still going to be strategic about their expansion, it was happening. The bird had left the nest.

CHAPTER 13

No "I" in Torchy's

A restaurant is as strong as the relationships behind it.

Austin, Texas, 2011. In the fall of 2011—five years after the hot August day when Mike served his first taco from the trailer—Torchy's was not only alive, its P&L margins were pretty stellar.

Mike had known all along what his odds were. He'd heard plenty of statistics—60 percent of restaurants shut down in their first year; 80 percent fold up shop before their fifth anniversary. So half a decade in, it felt like time to celebrate.

But even with so much momentum, there were still some significant changes, particularly behind the scenes. More stops and starts. Namely, Torchy's was facing a change in ownership.

Bob, for all his personality and sacrifice, was out. Though his contributions had no doubt helped carry the team in its first real run at expansion, it was clear that his season was ending. He was getting older, and the demands of the young company were never ending. It was time to slip into retirement again, for a second time.

Not wanting to leave the team in the lurch, Bob quietly sought out his replacement, and it seemed the answer was right in front of him, someone who was already invested in Torchy's—physically, emotionally, and even financially. Someone who was already part of the family: Alfonso Angelone, aka, Fonz.

So once again, the owners gathered at the long wooden table in the Kubena kitchen. While they were sad to lose a partner and a friend, they also realized that having Fonz as a replacement would make a bumpy transition as smooth as possible.

First of all, they wouldn't have to worry about an outsider coming in. Already, with their multi-owner platform, they were defying the odds. Just ask anyone. A five-owner model was a recipe for dissention and self-destruction. To get five heads of a company all functioning together in the first place was nothing short of a miracle, so the thought of replacing one of them this late in the game seemed tentative at best. Like the Jenga tower that tumbled down when you pulled out one block. But Fonz wasn't new. They'd worked with him. They knew they got along with him. It made a potentially huge transition seem not so bad.

Aside from the existing friendships, bringing Fonz on would also have some financial benefits. Rebecca, in particular, saw the opportunity as a way to streamline some of the company's debt. Finally, they were at a place where a reputable bank would give them a decent loan. They no longer needed to depend on personal investors for the capital to get started. They needed to start paying off some of those personal investments, and this provided them an opportunity to settle up some debt with Fonz and his family. Fonz could trade some of his initial investment in Torchy's locations for the capital to buy Bob out.

For the most part, the team decided that things would remain the same. They were going to continue self-governance as long as they could, each of them maintaining their individual silos of expertise. Mike, obviously, was head of culinary. Farrell was in charge of business development. Rebecca was chief of finance. Jay ran operations. Bob had been leading up the marketing, and since Fonz didn't have much experience in that area, he decided to focus on developing the IT department. Much of the marketing was going to digital/social media anyway. It seemed like the perfect fit.

Once the ownership switch was settled, it was business as usual. And business as usual, even though there was finally a surplus of cash coming in, still meant the doors were open seven days a week, 7:00 AM to 10:00 PM. With his busy and expanding company, Mike was watching his dream come true before his eyes, but the workload was a lot for one person.

In short, he was tired.

There were other stressors outside of work. He'd gotten to experience the great joy of becoming a new father, but shortly after it, he was dealing with the pangs of a failing marriage and impending divorce.

"You need help," Jay told Mike one afternoon. "It's time to hire a culinary director. I know you want to have control of the kitchen and make sure every bite on every plate is perfect, but you're just one person."

Mike rubbed the deepening creases in his forehead. "You're probably right."

"I'm definitely right. If we keep expanding like this, you're just going to wear out."

"It would have to be the perfect person, you know? Someone who really gets it. Who gets *me*."

"For sure. And I'm not saying do it right away. Take your time. Find that right person. But the responsibility needs to be shared."

That night, Mike came home late as usual. He crept inside, setting his keys on the table by the front door and slipping off his shoes. Once again, he'd been so busy making food all day that he'd hardly had time to eat, but as always, it was first things first. He tiptoed down the hallway and slowly opened the door.

A sliver of light cut the room, landing on the crib in the center of it, where Mike Jr. was sprawled out like a starfish, sound asleep. Almost two years old now, the toddler was doing new tricks every day. Like father, like son: as soon as he'd learned to walk, he was off to the races—always going as fast as he could, no fear of crashing. Mike saw so much of himself in the boy, it almost scared him, and he wondered if his own father had ever felt the same way, leaning over his crib a few decades earlier. Mike understood now some of the sacrifices his father had made for his career.

"Daddy loves you," Mike whispered, untwisting the blanket and covering the boy. He bent down and kissed his head. "Sleep tight."

He walked back down the hall and, too exhausted to make it to his own bed, he collapsed on the couch. Jay was right. He wasn't any good to anyone if he worked himself into the ground. Everyone was counting on him—Mike Jr. most of all.

I need help. But who?

He wanted a director of culinary, but he didn't know where to begin the search. The role was personal. Too intimate to simply put out an ad for it.

The partnership he sought in the kitchen had to be thought out if it was going to last. He knew that all too well.

And then it hit him—*I know who to call.*

It would be a long shot, but the chemistry was right. The talent was there. He almost couldn't wait until morning to call up an old friend.

MIKE'S FRIENDSHIP WITH CHERYL DRUMMOND began in 2002, at Spider House coffee shop in Austin. Fresh out of culinary school, Cheryl was attending her first real job interview. She was meeting Mike Rypka, the executive chef for Sodexo Corporation, for a catering job, and she was nervous as hell.

But after only a couple of minutes at the table with him, she was totally at ease. She found her potential new boss to be anything but intimidating. He had an easy manner about him. He asked a lot about her, like he was just trying to get to know her. They shared a lot of favorite foods and restaurants.

But Cheryl had promised herself that she wouldn't get swept away and forget what she came for—namely, income and stability. She'd paid her dues, and it was time to start making some money. To get paid what she deserved. As she sensed the interview was nearing an end, she decided it was time to play hardball.

"Well, Mr. Rypka."

"Mike."

"Well, Mike. Here's the thing. I need to make $13 an hour…and I'm afraid I can't back down from it."

Mike smiled and glanced down at her resume. "Well, I think we can work that out."

From that moment on, the relationship grew into a mentorship, and eventually, a close friendship. The two chefs worked hand in hand, until Mike transitioned from Sodexo to Lucy's Boatyard in hopes of more creative freedom.

Still, they stayed in touch. They ran into each other on the riverfront from time to time. They laughed, they caught up, occasionally Mike would share his hopes of opening his own restaurant.

"What about you?" he asked one afternoon. "How's it going in the corporate world?"

"Well, I got a promotion…They gave me your old job," Cheryl said. "I'm executive chef now."

Mike was genuinely happy for her. The corporate world didn't suit everyone, but Cheryl had met every challenge and distinguished herself in every crowd. Mike remembered the unsolicited advice he'd been given by Bryan Dolieslager at the Springfield Golf and Country Club about never staying somewhere too long, learning what you could and moving on, fast, to the next job. Mike decided to offer Cheryl his own and also unsolicited twist to Bryan's wisdom.

"Here's a little piece of advice," Mike said, "not that you've asked for it—but sometimes, if you stay with a company and move across the country, doors open up."

Over the next few months, she thought about Mike's advice a lot. Cheryl loved Austin, but he was right. A move made total sense.

Fast forward a few months, and she was in Boston, where she continued to climb the Sodexo ladder until she was wining and dining some of the most powerful people in the company and their invited guests.

Mike still called from time to time. He even pitched her his taco trailer idea—Little Devil logo and all.

Like many of Mike's closer friends, Cheryl expressed hesitation. "I think the taco concept is totally perfect for you, but just be careful, Mike. A trailer sounds like a lot of hard work without a lot of reward."

In total, it was an eight-year run in Boston. Cheryl's career had skyrocketed. She'd gotten married, and everything was great, but it had been a hard year. Both Cheryl and her wife, Rita, had had multiple family members—mothers, grandmothers, fathers, aunts and siblings—deal with major illnesses or pass away.

The end result: 15 trips back home to Texas. Cheryl and Rita both knew it was too much. As much as Cheryl loved the East Coast, they needed to go home.

So, reluctantly, they sold their condo in Boston. They had just packed the last box into the moving truck and Cheryl was rounding the empty bedroom doing one last check when her phone rang.

It was Mike.

The conversation that followed is what she still calls the craziest coincidence of her life.

"What are you up to?" Mike asked.

"Well, we're leaving Boston right now. We're moving home," Cheryl said, looking out the window. Her car was running, and Rita and the dogs were already inside it. She was fighting back tears. "I may need to call you back."

"Moving? Are you kidding me? Back to Austin?"

"Houston. Didn't you see my post on Facebook?"

"No. But, oh my God, Cheryl, you're not going to believe this. I need you."

"What are you talking about?"

"I'm ready for a director of culinary, darlin…for Torchy's. This thing has taken off, and I hate to say this, but I *really* need you. Just get to Houston and call me."

To Mike, it was already a done deal. Cheryl could not be more perfect for the job.

And again, the stars had aligned. The Torchy's team was just solidifying its next move into a new city. They'd gotten their footing in Dallas, so it was time for the next big Texas market: Houston, the unofficial restaurant capital of the Lone Star State. And as fate would have it, Cheryl was also moving there at the exact same time.

Mike met with each of the partners. He wanted Jay, specifically, to be on board with his potential new prospect.

"Dude, I know I told you to be picky, but this..." Jay scanned Cheryl's lengthy resume. "I haven't seen a resume this stacked since... ever."

"Yeah, she's been around. But I was her first boss out of culinary," Mike offered proudly.

"State Street Financial Center in Boston, and before that, she was hosting Michael Dell's top clients? Holy shit," Jay said, reading off her credentials. "She's never gonna go for it. And even if she did, we couldn't pay her *near* what she's worth."

"I know. But she's an old friend, and there are things we can offer her here beyond money."

"Of course. And I know you guys have a history, I'm just saying— she's big time."

"There won't be any hard feelings if she turns me down. I just got the keys to the new space on Shepherd Street, so I'm going to Houston tomorrow to meet her there."

The next day, just as planned, Cheryl met Mike at what would be the newest Torchy's location. Yet another good sign was that the house Rita and Cheryl had bought—before Mike had called—was in the very same neighborhood as the new restaurant. Cheryl could actually walk to where the new Torchy's would be.

But as they approached the empty building, it occurred to Mike that taking his potential new culinary partner to an old, vacated building he hadn't even seen wasn't exactly rolling out the red carpet.

"Probably should have scoped out the place before I asked you to join me," Mike said, unlocking the door and giving it a shove.

Walking into failed restaurants is like entering a city after a siege— the upturned tables, the random reams of cups, the dust and scattered remnants of a happier time. A time when there was music and laughter and dining.

"So the last guy here who went out of business…what was his operation?" Cheryl asked as the two of them looked over the abandoned kitchen equipment.

"A taco shop, actually," Mike laughed. "It was actually the third restaurant in a row to fail in this location," he added with a charming smile.

"Well, this is a great blender." Cheryl picked up one of the industrial units used for making daiquiris.

"Take it. We don't have a bar or any use for that anyway."

Cheryl put the blender down. "Look, Mike, I'll be honest for a second. Things are going well at Torchy's. I can see that."

"Yeah. We're still far from Easy Street, but it's definitely gaining steam."

"I've tasted your food. And I have no doubt in my mind that even though all these other guys have failed here, you'll be successful. But you're killing yourself."

"Nah. Not any more than anyone else."

"I don't think that's true. And you know it. That's why you called me. And I want to be there for you. I was so sorry when I heard about your divorce."

"Yeah, well," Mike said, brushing it off. "Shit happens."

"I want to help you take care of your son…so here's what I propose."

"Okay…"

"You get moved into this store and let me get moved into my house, and we'll talk about it again."

By the time of the launch party for the Torchy's on Shepherd Street, Cheryl's decision hadn't officially been made, but everything in her heart told her it was a go.

She and Rita arrived at the opening party not knowing quite what to expect, but as they approached the building, they felt the music pulsing down the street underneath their feet before they even arrived.

"A DJ and a keg?" Rita looked at Cheryl.

"I'm not surprised. They know how to throw a party."

Cheryl had attended countless corporate events, but nothing like this. The energy was electric. Members of the Torchy's crew came up to her all night, introducing themselves.

"Do you see what I'm talking about?" Cheryl turned to her wife at the end of the evening, her smile broadening. "This thing is special. You can't quite put your finger on it…I feel like I'm supposed to be a part of it, but—" Cheryl added tentatively, "I'll have to take a big pay cut—"

"I get it." Rita nodded. She knew it too. She'd already seen enough coincidences to acknowledge Torchy's was meant to be. She also knew when her wife was inspired. "Of course, you're going to do this."

"And the pay cut?"

"Who cares?" Rita shrugged. "Anyway, I got a feeling this will turn out in the long run. Maybe better than you'd ever planned."

CHAPTER 14

Houston, We Have a Problem

Carry the big stick...Sometimes you'll use it.

Houston, 2012. Though the job offer was essentially a spit-in-the-hand agreement, from day one, Cheryl threw herself into the work.

Something in her gut told her Rita was right—this partnership was going to be for the long haul.

Once her decision was official, Mike made Cheryl a promise. "Look, I know you're not making what you're worth, but you have my word, as soon as I can pay you more—I will."

Cheryl laughed. "May have to raise the price of your queso...oooh, or maybe you should try adding a bar?"

"Noted. But I mean it. I'm gonna take care of you. In the meantime, I got you this." Mike reached behind his back and hefted a large cardboard box.

Cheryl reached inside the box and pulled out the industrial blender she'd admired the day they scoped out the new restaurant location.

"Pretty sure it still works," Mike added.

"You shouldn't have." Cheryl accepted the heavy blender like a bouquet. "But for real—I *really* wanted this."

As the new head of kitchen, Cheryl's role was to standardize the recipes, so in the two weeks that followed, she and Mike hunkered down at Arbor Trails. They chose that location in part because Mike's star prep cook, Edith Nieto, was needed to help them determine the easiest and most efficient way of preparing menu items.

"Here you go," Mike said, handing Cheryl the book of recipes, all grimy and splattered with years of sauce.

"Almost like your grandmother's cookbook, ya know?" Cheryl looked at Edith who nodded politely. Cheryl thumbed through the recipe binder. The yellowed pages were falling out, and notes were scribbled in the oil-blotched margins. "There aren't even any pictures… This is what you cook from?"

Edith shrugged.

Cheryl turned to Mike. "Look, this is cool. Needs to be in some kind of Torchy's museum, but you have *13* restaurants now. We have to get organized."

"Absolutely." Mike slapped the binder. "Let's make this shit professional."

"Okay, so what we need is a master list—a Taco Bible, if you will."

"Taco Bible—like it!" Mike examined a bunch of cilantro and began chopping.

Cheryl's adrenaline was flowing now. The years of corporate training had made her perfect for this role. The more disorganized the situation, the more she shined. Torchy's had already been wildly successful— opening a dozen profitable stores—despite its helter-skelter mode of operation. She knew that was, in part, because the owners had poured their hearts into training. The owners stayed involved, and thanks to a little luck, so far, they'd managed to get things right. Torchy's had nothing resembling a corporate manual, and yet, the vibe, the food, even the heart had moved with them from location to location, city to city.

As Cheryl and Mike had discussed on the drive over from Houston, the ultimate goal was for anyone off the street to be able to look at a page from the Taco Bible, execute the recipe and the end product taste the same in Austin, Dallas—wherever.

"I'm assuming we'll want to prepare and photograph every recipe…" Cheryl said, "and we'll need to list every piece of equipment needed… record all details regarding prep, temperature, and presentation…"

A few days into making the Taco Bible, Mike turned to Cheryl. "Give it to me straight. What are our blind sides? What can be better?"

Cheryl shrugged. "It's pretty damn tasty—all of it."

"You're my director of culinary. Be critical."

Cheryl thought a minute. "Well, the rice could have a little more flavor, so...maybe we try a new base?"

"Okay, okay, I'm open to that. What else?"

"Black beans. They're a staple, but maybe they could have a little more punch?"

"Now we're talking, girl!"

"And once the menu is standardized, we'll need to implement some safety standards."

Mike popped a grilled shrimp into his mouth. "Oh, for sure."

"I can visit each of the locations...do some safety audits," Cheryl said. Her time in the corporate world had made her good at spotting a liability. Mike shared the same corporate background, but the truth was, he just hadn't had a second to think about it.

Mike winked at Edith and slapped her on the back. "See! *That's* why she's here!"

Cheryl's strengths went far beyond standardization. What she also brought to the team, particularly the new crew members, was an understanding of hospitality that had been forged in the fires of some high-stakes (and quite frankly, badass) corporate dinners.

As she put it, "Spend years serving lobster foie gras to execs from around the world and you come away with nerves of steel."

Cheryl had fed, entertained, and hosted the "biggest of the big" in the business world, and her simple takeaway was this: *Never let them see you sweat.* She joked that her role was a glorified form of babysitting, but the truth was, she had guts.

Which, quite honestly, was another characteristic she and Mike shared. He, too, never shied away from high stakes…and he would prove it after the opening in Houston on Shepherd Street.

THINGS WERE GOING WELL in Houston. Even though they'd done this a dozen times, Farrell still got nervous and Mike was still surprised when the lines curled around the building and down the block.

But two weeks after the opening, something happened. Something awful. Something that could have stopped the speeding taco train right there in its tracks.

Torchy's got a bad review.

To make matters worse, the review was from a well-known food critic: two-time James Beard award winner Alison Cook.

It wasn't just that Ms. Cook had gotten a bad meal at the new location in Houston, the tone of her review, published in the *Houston Chronicle,* made her lunch experience sound less like disappointment and more like a personal assault.

And to some extent, it was. It was an attack on her memory. On the perfect taco she'd eaten in Austin some months back. She was at the original Torchy's location, and there, in the small patch of shade the trailer park provided, she had a life-altering moment with the Dirty Sanchez taco.

Since 2006, that taco, which bears the name of an Urban Dictionary term for a sex act, had been a favorite at every location. It was a breakfast home run: scrambled eggs with a fried poblano chile, guacamole, escabeche carrots, and shredded cheese, served with Poblano sauce on a fresh flour tortilla.

But Ms. Cook claimed that the taco she had in Houston couldn't hold a candle to the one she had first ordered in Austin. As she said in her scathing review, "the magic got lost in translation."

Her main beef was with the service. A zealous floor manager, for some reason, was dead set on taking Ms. Cook's menu from the table, even after she expressed her desire to keep it. Her other qualm was with the tortilla, which was not made in-house. From the beginning, Mike had wanted to make his own tortillas, but starting a restaurant in a trailer meant that space was limited. So Mike did the next best thing: he found a local company that made high-quality tortillas delivered daily. In fact, the tortillas were so fresh that when they were dropped off at the stores, the boxes were usually still hot.

But on that day in Houston, Ms. Cook was sorely disappointed with the Dirty Sanchez, calling the taco on Shepherd Street "a washed-out shadow of what I remembered."

Then, as often happens when you mix anonymity with misguided passion, a verbal war broke out. In the online comments below Ms. Cook's review, the feud became less about food and more of a larger, "which city is better—Austin vs. Houston" brawl.

For some restaurant owners, some with less gumption (and less confidence in their product), that kind of critique could have been the turning point that took the whole thing down. A tremor that would spread through the new location and even the psyche of the Torchy's team.

Mike had been in the game long enough to know you take the good with the bad. There would inevitably be "off" days, particularly when a store is new. He understood that his food wasn't going to blow everyone's mind, every time. He also knew that sometimes in the service industry, someone is going to get rubbed the wrong way.

But, Mike was willing to go to bat for his product, and the poor review, quite frankly, wasn't going to have the last word. So, he did the only thing he could think to do. He, himself, responded in the comments in an effort to make things right:

THE GODS HAVE SPOKEN! Thank you, Alison, for ripping apart my restaurant!....To be honest, the Damn in me wants to tell all the haters F@#& off, but the Good in me knows that the people's opinion counts. It's easy to rant and rave online and behind closed doors. I'm not saying the experience [you] had at my restaurant was untrue. No one is perfect, believe me. Perhaps we had an employee that had his head up his own A@& that day. Trust me, anyone who owns a restaurant knows how hard it is to run one. That's precisely why so many fail. The biggest problem I have with this review is not the comments, but the fact that it's awful hard to fix the situation if we can't get details about the very thing that upset them. I'd very much like to address the individual in the scenario, but can't seem to point the pitchfork in the right direction. As far as our food goes— some love us, some hate us. Our tortillas aren't home cooked because I didn't have the space in the trailer we started in.

In fact, to demonstrate our care, please note that I'll be at the Shepherd location tomorrow afternoon (4/27) from 11a-2p. I'll be giving away FREE Dirty Sanchezs to anyone who prints out this article and brings it in. After you eat the taco, I'd like to know if you agree with Ms. Cook or not. We love all of our customers and for those who have had bad experiences, I deeply apologize. I hope that you'll take this opportunity and let us win you back!

He ended his quasi-rant with his signature confidence: *See you tomorrow, folks!*

Mike went home that night, packed a small duffel bag, and got on the road to Houston so that in the morning, when the doors opened on Shepherd Street, he would be there—bright-eyed, freshly shaven, and ready to meet his guests.

As he had done with past endeavors that involved his restaurant, Mike didn't allow himself to go down the path of self-doubt: *Am I inviting more trouble? What if people don't show up?*

There was no time for that. Twitter was just six years old. It wasn't commonplace for chefs to publicly defend their restaurants from a food critic's negative review. Again, Mike was ahead of the curve. Consequences be damned.

But if he was honest, something deep in his gut told him—as it had so many times before—that he just had one thing to focus on. One job.

Make good food and people will come.

By the next morning, the comments thread on Ms. Cook's review was long enough to span the distance from Houston to Austin. Torchy's faithfuls had come to Mike's defense, calling Ms. Cook's article a blasphemy and pledging to show up at the new location at 11 o'clock sharp.

Mike and Fonz tied on their aprons and watched as the crowd swelled outside. A couple of the patrons were even dressed as devils, makeshift pitchforks in hand. All of them hungry and waiting to prove Ms. Cook wrong.

"F that food critic!" someone shouted as they unlocked the glass doors and the people poured in. "Houston has been waiting for you guys!"

Everyone on the Torchy's team had hoped the fans would show in support, but what they hadn't expected was the half dozen news vans circling the crowded parking lot.

"I think every news station in Texas wants to talk to you, Mike," Fonz said, shaking his head.

Again, there wasn't time to plan. Mike had to act in the moment, and he had to speak from the heart.

"I know I've turned into mama bear here," he told one reporter, "but I felt like the review was a little unfair. I stand behind our brand and our product, and while Ms. Cook is entitled to her opinion, I wasn't going to let that be the last word. I'd like people to decide for themselves."

After a day of recording-breaking sales and hugs and photos, Fonz and Mike slumped down, exhausted. The masses had come. And the Torchy's team had not only fed them, but they'd also made new fans.

"You're totally fearless, dude," Fonz said. "I mean, for real, you got balls."

Mike shrugged. It was the first time he'd ever taken on a negative review. And likely the last, but he was proud. Satisfied.

"Well you know what they say, man," Mike laughed. "No such thing as bad press."

THE FIVE OWNERS MIGHT have had differing opinions about a lot of stuff, but even after the hiccup in Houston, one thing they were all certain about was their desire to expand. They believed in Torchy's. They knew it was bigger than just food, and they felt they owed it to their guests (and to themselves) to keep growing. To take the food—and the opportunities with it—to the next level.

Even though Torchy's wasn't yet a household name outside of Texas, the owners were often surprised by the recognition their little company had garnered. If Mike or Jay started making small talk with the person next to them on an airplane, the response was often: "You're with Torchy's? I *love* that place! We can't wait till you come to our town."

But some of the taco fanatics were not really okay with the long game. They'd visited Austin, they'd been wooed by the queso, and they wanted it in their hometown—*now*. And they were willing to do some strange things to get just that.

There was that one afternoon when a member of the team came to the back office and tapped on the open door. "Mike," she said. "Someone's here to see you."

"Okay but if it's anyone wanting to be paid, tell them to hang on a sec," Mike said, rifling through the papers on his desk. "I'm looking for this invoice…"

"I don't think they want money," she said tentatively. "Just come see this."

Mike put the stack of papers down and followed her out to the foyer where a woman stood smiling. She wore a striped outfit. Her face was painted orange and her shoulder-length wig was green. Anyone who had grown up watching *Willie Wonka & the Chocolate Factory* recognized her outfit at once.

"Are you an Oompa—"

The woman cut off Mike's question, answering it with her song:

"*Oompa Loompa doopity doo.*
I've got a perfect puzzle for you.
Where should the next Torchy's be?
If you are wise, you'll listen to me."

By now, other employees had gathered and were listening to the singing telegram.

"What the hell?" Mike whispered.

"*Oompa Loompa doopity doe...*

Please bring Torchy's to CO-LO-RA-DO!" the woman sang, punctuating the crescendo with the splits.

Unfortunately, the answer was no. Colorado would come in due time, but at that moment, there was a process, and after several long talks with Rebecca and Jay, Mike realized the next step was a human resources department.

The more the team grew, the more they spread themselves out. And the more people that were under their care, the greater the liability. The risk had grown such that Mike almost couldn't sleep at night. The creation of an HR department would be yet another significant milestone for the small team. A necessity. A hallmark of a legitimate company.

They'd just recently moved their makeshift office from a shared room at the trailer park to a little building on Heather Street. With some dividers and creative engineering, they'd made four cubicles where there should have been one, and there, Mike, Rebecca, Jay, Fonz, and Farrell each had a few feet of office space.

Like siblings sharing a room, of course there was the occasional bickering. But overall, they were insanely lucky that they'd been able to self-govern for so long. For the most part, from the top down, the company had not needed outside intervention to mediate its problems.

Still, they all knew it was necessary to form an HR department, even if the move felt so…corporate.

After much research, Jay hired a woman with an HR background who wedged herself into the spare chair at the tiny office and began her preliminary discovery.

"Tell me about Torchy's protocol regarding catering drivers?" Her hair was slicked back and her suit pressed.

"Well," Jay chuckled, slightly embarrassed. "We give them a gas card."

She raised her eyebrows.

"You know…so they don't have to pay for gas themselves."

"Okay," she scribbled on a notebook. "Guess that's a start. And safety standards?"

"We've actually been developing those with our new head of culinary. She worked for Marriott."

"That will definitely help. And regarding new store openings…the keg parties…and shooting tacos out of a cannon. Probably gonna need to make some tweaks there."

"We gotta keep the cannon. It's kind of our trademark."

"Sure, but you'll have to shoot something out of it that won't get hot sauce in someone's eye."

"That's fair," Jay said.

"You hired me to be the bad guy. I personally love Torchy's, but you guys should count yourselves *very* lucky to have so many locations and so few issues." She shook her head. "You beat some odds."

Jay shrugged. "You know what they say: you don't need an HR department until you have one."

"Let's hope that's not the case."

The HR department was a milestone, but just around the corner was another one. A much bigger leap. One that would require months—then years—of preparation, and the bulk of that prep would fall on the strong shoulders of someone who was 5'4".

Rebecca Kubena, who years before had been selling suitcases to department stores and boasted no MBA, was going to lead their little company into the wilds of equity financing.

PART THREE

CHAPTER 15

"The Jets Are Lining the Runway"

Don't be afraid to go big.

Austin, 2016. The first time that Jay Sonner ever heard of Torchy's Tacos was from Michelle, the boisterous office administrator at North Point Advisors where he worked as a managing director. Around the office, Michelle was known for two things: 1) her powerful voice, and 2) her longtime role as right-hand of David Jacquin, the company's founder and CEO.

"Fair-elle or maybe it was Far-elle…" Michelle said, butchering the name on her sticky note. "His last name was Bean something…maybe it was Pharrell Bean…I don't know, he was talking so fast."

Jay's ears perked up.

David, his boss, chimed in, "Can you qualify this for us a little bit, Michelle? Torchy's is a…?"

"Restaurant. In Austin," Michelle nodded. "And this Pharrell person said he was inviting you to Texas to see them."

David nodded, acknowledging he'd heard the message and then ducked his head back down into whatever paperwork was in front of him. At the end of the last recession, his investment bank, North Point Advisors Inc., had enjoyed a big run. Huge, in fact. People in the financial world were starting to see the value created in consumer multi-units, specifically restaurants, which are an $860-billion market in the U.S. today. In 2015, when Farrell Kubena of Torchy's Tacos first called the office and spoke with Michelle, North Point was killing it. Their average deal size was $350 to $400 million. (To date, it's the biggest consumer merger and acquisition practice in the country.)

Needless to say, Michelle, and the rest of the folks in the office, were fielding a lot of calls. And so, David wasn't necessarily moved to action by a taco restaurant in Texas (that he'd never heard of) represented by some man whose name no one could pronounce.

Fast forward a few weeks, and David and Jay were in the company airplane headed to Manhattan. They were somewhere over the Midwest when Jay remembered the little taco company. *Torchy's*. Right away, the name of the place appealed to him. It was short, easy, catchy. It evoked a little mischief. He pulled up his phone and started scrolling through the Yelp reviews. The photos of the food, no doubt, looked amazing. Not your typical pile of shredded lettuce and guac hedged by a wall of refried beans. It was artistic, fresh. *Jamaican jerked chicken…fried avocado.* The more he read, the hungrier he got.

From the photos, he gathered that the décor was also unique. None of the indoor spaces looked the same. The interiors were bold and industrial, yet warm and inviting.

But it was the fans that Jay found particularly compelling. They didn't just rave, they gushed.

TORCHY'S!!! When are you guys coming to Alabama?

Three words: QUESO, QUESO, QUESOOOOOOOO. Best I've ever had—no doubt.

I don't go for Tex-Mex that's not traditional, but let me tell you, Torchy's changed that! I drive 45 minutes into Houston just to get it.

He checked Instagram and Facebook and found more of the same. Torchy's didn't just have fans, they had *superfans*.

For tacos? Jay was pretty impressed. It was also clear that none of this was constructed from the inside. The iPhone shots of the baja shrimp and some pork taco smothered in queso—the reviewer called it "trashy"—were all coming from "real people." Totally organic.

Even though he'd taken about a hundred of these calls that month alone, after reading the feedback, it was clear that Torchy's answered the threshold questions Jay asked of every potential client.

Is the brand bigger than the store portfolio?

Is it bigger than its own physical footprint?

After just a few minutes on social media, the answer was a resounding yes.

"Looks like a winner," Jay said to his boss, handing over his iPhone so David could see for himself. "And I'm starving now."

David shrugged. "If you think so, let's do it. Let's stop off in Austin and see this thing."

"Now?" Jay said. "Austin isn't on the way to New York."

"If Torchy's is as hot as you say, a detour will pay us back in spades. We can be there by lunch."

When the company plane touched down at Austin-Bergstrom International Airport, Farrell Kubena was already there waiting. He'd gotten the call from Jay Sonner, who was rerouting the North Point jet to follow up on Farrell's cold call.

"Hell yeah!" Farrell said when he hung up the phone. "The big boys have come a-courtin'!" He grabbed his keys and climbed into his Mercedes G-Wagon and headed towards the airport to greet them.

Immediately, Jay liked Farrell's vibe. He was confident yet approachable. His energy was off the charts. He talked ninety-to-nothing, speeding towards the Torchy's headquarters in East Austin. Jay wasn't super familiar with the city, but he knew that where they were headed was sort of the boonies. Not a C-suite downtown.

Farrell turned the Benz into a driveway in front of a chain-linked fence draped with barbed wire. "Here we are."

He punched a code on the keypad, and the gate opened. High in the crystal blue Texas sky above them was a spinning globe, and a caricature of a wild-eyed baby devil in a diaper glared down.

"'Torchy's *World* Headquarters?'" Jay laughed at the bravado.

"That's right," Farrell said. "Texas was just the beginning. We've got big plans."

The one-level building was cool but definitely unassuming. Farrell showed them around the office. "It was a former city building. Urban legend is that they used this space to monitor roadkill, among other things," Farrell said. "You know—to make sure it didn't have any diseases or anything."

"Well," David said politely. "I'd say you've made some improvements."

Farrell ended the tour in the Founders Lounge which was an open room with chairs scattered around.

"Here's the gang." Farrell stepped aside so that Jay Sonner and David could see the rest of the ownership team. "This is Mike Rypka, the man behind the madness. This is my lovely wife, Rebecca, who keeps us all in check. Jay Wald, our head of operations, and Alfonso Angelone, our technology director. You can call him Fonz."

"There are...five of you?" Jay Sonner asked.

"Yep," Farrell said. "Let's get down to business."

After everyone took their seats, Farrell began. "We've been getting calls from all over the country...private equity groups, venture capital firms...We've been putting them off for a long time, but now we're finally ready to talk. We're doing $5 million volumes in our new stores."

At that number, both David and Jay sat up in their chairs.

"It's time to plan for the future. And we need the best people in the business to tell us how to do that."

The meeting, albeit brief, was beyond fortuitous. David and Jay had assumed that Torchy's was profitable, but after a brief peek under the tent, they were floored. The Little Devil was outpunching its weight class ten to one. They'd done the hard part without any kind of financial backing. With a little guidance, Jay knew Torchy's tacos would sell—and sell big.

"Thank you, guys, for taking the time to stop by. I think North Point and Torchy's are a good fit," Farrell said as he drove the men back to the airport. Clearly, he was trying to gauge their reaction. He knew what he had was special. And now, the folks at North Point also knew it was special. He was curious—all of the owners were curious—*how would a market situation reward them for creating something so exceptional?*

"Jay will be back next week," David said as they shook hands on the tarmac. "Let's hit the ground running."

The race was on.

As promised, Jay returned to Austin the next week. He checked into the Saint Cecilia Hotel, a hip bohemian bungalow in the South Congress district. He would stay there weeks, eating tacos and immersing himself in the culture of his favorite new client. When Torchy's opened its new locations, Jay traveled for the launch parties, each time feeling a bit like an anthropologist observing this strange tribe of taco-loving people who exude energy.

At one of the openings, Jay sat outside, and though he was not a smoker, he tried to puff on the cigar Mike had given him. As he watched the line of patrons grasping at t-shirts fired from the old taco cannon, he laughed. "These people are nuts," he said to himself.

There was no better way to describe it.

Six weeks later, all of what Jay observed was wedded with the financials to create what is known in the merger & acquisitions world as the CIM, or Confidential Information Memorandum. This book of marketing materials (pronounced "sim") would be used to woo potential investors. This was Jay's job, to somehow capture a company's *raison d'etre*, its core, its essence. He knew that Torchy's was special, and therefore the Torchy's CIM would have to reflect that. The typical black and whites of a standard executive summary wouldn't do. It needed to be quirky, and original and full of heart, like the company it represented.

To that end, Jay made sure the CIM included little caveats. *We have a secret menu,* it read. One might assume this secret menu would be included, but instead there was an asterisk and a note at the bottom. *What is it? We can't tell you—It's a secret!*

There was also a level of urgency to Jay's work. He needed to present the companies he represented in such a way that investors saw them as stars on the rise. He needed them to know that what they were privy to was going to be the next big thing. The time to act was now. But with Torchy's, there was no need to construct the narrative. It was unfolding in real time. When a restaurant gets crazy mobs at its very front door, it's just a matter of snapping a photograph. A picture is worth a thousand bar graphs, especially as far as the CIM was concerned.

Things were already coming together nicely, and then President Barack Obama stopped off at the El Paso Street location during the drafting process. He ordered two tacos: the Republican and the Democrat (naturally) and shook hands with the starstruck Torchy's crew—both front and back of the house. The photo of Obama smiling with the Torchy's GM was smack in the middle of the CIM. This thing wasn't just cool, it was Obama-level cool. Torchy's really was the taco rocket, like everyone said.

A year and a half of work later, it was all there, bound up into the thick, marketing document.

Now to see who would bite.

ANDREW CRAWFORD KNEW A winner when he saw one. Even before he'd joined up with the global growth equity investor General Atlantic to start their consumer group, he'd been able to sniff out success. He'd cut his teeth on some heavy hitters, among them, Bojangles and lululemon athletica (when it was just a little Canadian apparel retailer with only three stores in the United States). In short, Crawford had good instincts. So when he came across a little quirky taco restaurant that was making waves in Austin, Texas, Crawford's sixth sense told him to go after them.

On paper, Torchy's didn't pose much of a risk. At General Atlantic, the objective was simply to put capital to work. And to do that, they needed to identify fast-growing companies and then get those companies to take their money. One of their company directives was this: *find companies that win with revenue*. When Crawford flipped through the book of marketing materials and saw the images of people waiting outside Torchy's front door, he didn't need spreadsheets to tell him that their sales per unit was off the charts.

Moreover, Crawford was no stranger to the taco concept. His wife's family owned a chain of Mi Cocinas in Dallas. Mi Cocina was in a different class of restaurant than Torchy's (they were more "casual dining"), but thanks to his in-laws, Crawford knew the taco business was what he called a "sneaky" category. And by "sneaky" he meant surprisingly profitable. Already General Atlantic had invested in a taco concept called Bartaco, and it had proven to be a quick success.

What Crawford also found interesting was that Torchy's was even more successful *beyond* the borders of Texas. Tex-Mex is notorious for performing poorly outside its region. It's one thing to have a successful restaurant concept in Austin. Three or four locations perform locally, and one might think: *it's an Austin thing*. But what if you moved it across Texas—Dallas, Fort Worth, Houston, San Antonio? And then exported it across the state line?

As far as he could tell, Torchy's was doing better in Colorado than it was in its home state of Texas. It already had proven portability.

Shaw Joseph was Crawford's partner on the deal. Crawford had brought Joseph to the company to head up General Atlantic's restaurant division, so it was Joseph's job to do the legwork when they had a lead.

As always, Joseph did his research. He polled all the experts. "What are the best, fastest growing companies out there?"

The answer, of course, involved some of the usual suspects: Chick-fil-A, Raising Cane's, In & Out Burger, Whataburger, particularly its Texas presence. But the one restaurant that people really seemed most excited to talk about was Torchy's Tacos.

Even though he was paid to be an optimist, Joseph had learned to keep his enthusiasm in check. In this business, restaurants, in particular, were especially risky. For one thing, the barriers to entry are very low. Everybody's got a buddy in the restaurant business, and most of the time that poor sap is working his butt off while losing his shirt—even if the food is good. What Torchy's had done in creating a concept *ex nihilo* that had grown to 40 successful units was just unheard of. More than that, the brand clearly resonated with consumers. So much so that when a new store opened, people were lining up around the block in a blizzard to get a free taco that's worth $3.50.

"We've gotta talk to Torchy's," Crawford told Joseph. "They've got a half dozen owners, just get one of them to take a call."

"I'm trying."

For weeks, Joseph did his best to reach out—emails, cold calls, FedEx. He'd guessed at Mike Rypka's email address. A time or two he'd managed to get a cordial response, something like: *we appreciate your inquiry, but at this time, we are not interested.* Joseph wondered if the team thought he was seeking to franchise them. If he could just explain, they might see how General Atlantic could be the right fit.

Months later, he got a hit. His efforts were finally rewarded when one of his many emails somehow got forwarded on to Jay Sonner at North Point, and finally, Sonner reached out to schedule a meeting.

The timing—on July 5—wasn't exactly ideal, but the General Atlantic guys had been waiting so long for an introduction, they were happy to cut their holiday short. Joseph and Crawford along with GA advisor Todd Diener (a former president of Chili's restaurants) were in Austin the morning after Independence Day.

The meeting was unusual for many reasons. First, the location—in the Founders Lounge of the Torchy's World Headquarters—was as relaxed as the owners themselves. Instead of a boardroom table, there was a hodgepodge of modern furniture arranged in a circle. The men in their starched suits took their seats in the lounge chairs, and Joseph tried to figure out what to do with his legs.

Jay Sonner was the emcee of the deal, but when it came time to talk about goals, Mike explained the reason they all were there. "This thing is busting at the seams. We're ready to scale, but we know it's beyond us now. We want to attract a good CEO to help us do that, and we need outside investors to make us competitive. Basically, we are looking for some guidance to help us professionalize."

This kind of thing was exactly what the men from General Atlantic wanted to hear. This was their wheelhouse. Crawford pled the company's case: "Eighty percent of the $24 billion we invest is in non-control situations. That's not a mandate, that's just how it's worked out. We want you guys to keep the reins. We have operational experts—in

175

technology or marketing or whatever—that can help you as you scale. That's what we do best."

He tried not to sound overzealous. This was another way in which the meeting was unusual. Companies were typically trying to attract interest from General Atlantic, not the other way around. Owners would flex some muscles on paper, throw out some stats, hoping those numbers would raise eyebrows and secure them a deal.

But the Torchy's team was clearly not into all that. They were cool, yet down to earth and personable. Crawford and Joseph were pleasantly surprised by the unassuming people behind the machine. It was like when someone peels open the trench coat in a cartoon, and instead of an adult, you realize it's five kids stacked on top of each other. Ten minutes into that meeting on July 5, the GA team had decided they were willing to bet on those "kids." All five of them.

Around the General Atlantic offices, both Crawford and Joseph had the reputation of being conservative for their line of work. As they saw it, not every business was worth writing in lights and not every popular restaurant was a long-term hit. But Torchy's was different. The brand evoked that adrenaline rush of discovery that had gotten both men into the business in the first place.

In Crawford's mind, the five-owner aspect of the company was the only cause for concern. It was hard enough to please one person, but five times that?

But during the meeting, Torchy's team seemed to be on the same page. And that, in Crawford's mind, was largely to Mike's credit. As he saw it, Mike was the antithesis of the mercurial founder. He was even-keel and deferential when it came to the other partners. Crawford would later claim that Mike was humbler than any other owner he'd come across in his entire career.

The next step was to get the greenlight from everyone else on the General Atlantic board so they could secure the deal before someone else did. The secret was out. The G4s were lining the runway at Austin Executive, and two words were on everyone's lips: *Torchy's Tacos.*

Investors would be flying in. Like the mating ritual of a South American bird—the show, the dance, the trill—they'd vie for Torchy's attention and would not stop until one of them won out.

On the day of General Atlantic's quarterly global investment committee meeting, Crawford and Joseph tried to stay calm. The meeting, which was held in a high-rise in Midtown Manhattan, was where they presented the three or four businesses that they wanted to invest in.

The five partners (who would ultimately make the decision) took their places around a 10x20 conference table. Behind them, a wall of screens where 60-plus partners from 14 global offices were listening in.

There were a few companies on the agenda, but when it came time to present Torchy's, the energy was as close as it gets (in the executive world) to fever pitch.

"There's no need to overcomplicate this," Joseph said after he had gone over the preliminary info. "Torchy's has potential to be a big business. The sheer volume they are doing is bigger than anything we've ever seen at their price point, except for maybe Chick-fil-A. I mean look at a company like Chipotle—it's doing two-thirds of the business Torchy's is doing. Torchy's has higher volumes than Shake Shack, aside from its New York City location. If Torchy's only achieves a fraction of these potential outcomes, it's going to be a successful deal for us."

"I have yet to say this about any other company in my career," Crawford chimed in, "but we think this could potentially be a twenty-percent grower over the next couple of decades."

They concluded, and the room sat in silence. Torchy's should have been a done deal, still, Crawford and Joseph had both pitched some sure-fire prospects over the years and nobody had taken a swing.

But at that moment, everyone at General Atlantic, in person and on the screen, was listening.

The votes from the partners came in—one, two, three, four thumbs up. Bill Ford, General Atlantic's CEO, was the last to respond.

"Start the Torchy's CEO search tomorrow." He took off his glasses. "Get this deal done. Go after it with all you got."

CHAPTER 16

"The Core Fifty-Five"

Advice for someone who's hit the jackpot? Give it away.

Austin, 2017. The CIM that Jay Sonner of North Point Advisors crafted had been in heavy circulation. Of the 44 financial institutions that were approached regarding Torchy's, 42 of them took the marketing materials, and of those, 22 put in bids.

Jay had called it—Torchy's wasn't just a hit or home run. It was a grand slam.

For the sake of time and mental energy, the team collectively winnowed the pool down to ten, and after yet another round of intense meetings, all ten of the financial parties rebid. Jay and David's fortuitous last-minute plane detour to Austin had resulted in an investor response that was in the top one percent of businesses they worked with.

Mike was in disbelief. His company was in an auction process with some of the most sophisticated financial partners in the world. But Farrell just laughed. "I told you, Rypka—this thing is big."

All of this was happening because the owners had agreed it was time to take some money off the table. Everything they had was tied up in the company, and while they'd been okay with that for a time, they knew that once their heads were above water, it would be foolish not to diversify.

There was also the issue of scaling the business. The ragtag team had carried their baby devil further than anyone had ever dreamed. But now, Torchy's was bigger than they were, and in order to move into the next phase, they'd have to bring on some help. They'd muscled the company from nothing to 40 stores, but why stop there when there was potential for a thousand of them?

For that kind of expansion, they'd have to revisit the infrastructure. For starters, they needed a legitimate CEO. The way they all saw it, Torchy's was like a kid whose father coached him in baseball. The father loves his son and the game, and for a while, they are the perfect team. The kid excels—through T-ball, high school, maybe even college— because his dad dedicates all his time to the son's game. But at some point, the kid's potential exceeds the dad's resources. And for the love of his son—and respect for what he can achieve—the dad brings on a coach who is better equipped. In Torchy's case, that coach was an equity group.

Rebecca, for her own part, was down the rabbit hole of paperwork as she had been for almost a year. Torchy's financials were antiquated to say the least. They'd moved beyond hand-writing tickets, but not by much. Her job was to take the raw data and get it all into some sort of language that the modern financial world could understand. But Rebecca, by her own admission, was in over her head. "I haven't looked at the business like North Point looks at the business...or how the equity people will be looking at the business. I'm not an MBA, for crying out loud! My background is in sales."

But as she had always done before, instead of wasting time complaining, she went about figuring out how to achieve the desired result. For months, Rebecca excavated sales reports, extracting data and then transferring that data into Excel spreadsheets. All so that she could then hand those spreadsheets over to a team of very analytical 25-year-olds who'd never even seen a business that wasn't conceived in an MBA test tube.

The process of choosing the right partner, even with the help of North Point, was surreal and stressful. Aside from the owners, none of the Torchy's staff knew about the impending deal. Mike and the gang had kept it all hush-hush, conducting meeting after meeting in the Founders Lounge, a private office in the back of the headquarters that even had its own separate door. It was there that the owners debated the fate of the defunct bar-b-que trailer that had somehow turned into a multi-million-dollar asset.

Some days they would all flop down in the chairs. "This is the right decision," they'd say to each other.

The very next day they'd flop down into those same chairs. "What the hell are we doing?" they asked. "How's this going to shake out?"

Yes, the money was enticing, but there was always the lingering question: *What will it cost us?*

Of course they weren't talking about money. Torchy's wasn't just an investment, it was a mosaic of all five of them. Their blood and tears— their very own glued fingerprints. They'd given their lives to it. Would its essence be lost after such an enormous shift?

"What if we keep pushing this thing until it breaks?" Rebecca asked at one of the team meetings.

Everyone looked around, first at each other, then at Mike. "I don't know if we're prepared to handle this," Mike said, "but we've gotta keep growing. Keep moving forward."

"What we have is special, but it's largely because we're in control of it. We're in completely unknown territory with this financial stuff." Rebecca sighed. "We don't know what we're getting into."

As he'd done so many times before, Mike shrugged and smiled his comforting smile. "If we'd waited until we had all the answers before we made a significant move, we'd still be grilling meats in the alley."

The rest of the group knew he was right. They weren't just coworkers or even a community—they were a family. They believed in what they were doing, and they knew that growth would require an inherent amount of risk.

They couldn't stop now. Torchy's deserved the Big Leagues.

AT THE END OF the day, it was the notion of a true partnership that led Mike and the rest of the owners to go with Joseph and Crawford and the team at General Atlantic. GA didn't want control; they wanted a partnership. What they were offering was exactly what Torchy's needed—and nothing more.

It didn't hurt that the General Atlantic team leaders were also Southerners. Andrew Crawford was from North Carolina, Shaw Joseph from Louisiana, and their advisor Todd Diener was a Texan, born and bred. There was a camaraderie that came with geography and a good-natured Southern drawl.

After a few months, they had a handshake on the high-level terms of the deal, and over the next few weeks, with the help of some lawyers from New York, they ironed out the details with taxes.

In sorting through old documents, Rebecca stumbled on an old projection she'd prepared for a loan officer back several years back. She read it aloud to Mike, "By 2014, we are going to have 20 stores and our sales are going to be $36,000. Our projected net income is going to be $4,000."

"Well, I guess we surpassed that," Mike laughed.

Back then, it was all about surviving. Wondering if the next month would find them finally in the black. Here they were, in October 2017, and the company had done far more than they dared dream three years before.

And Mike, who'd once been too broke to buy three sleeves of paper boats for his tacos, was taking the largest check he'd ever seen and putting it in the bank.

ONCE THE DEAL WAS complete and the money was distributed, it was time to do the thing that all the owners had been waiting for—give it away.

This had perhaps excited them most. Mike and Jay Wald specifically, having been lifers in the restaurant industry (a stereotypically "dead-end" line of work), had always made it a point to take care of their people along the way. Many of their employees were young. They didn't worry about things like retirement, so Jay helped advocate for enriching Torchy's benefits with things like a 401k match. "This is one way we can be stewards for them," Jay had said.

But after the equity deal, it was time to take it to the next level. So many people—from dishwashers, to managers, to cashiers—had sacrificed to get Torchy's off the ground. Mike and the rest of the team knew that their success was the age-old thousand points of light. A culmination of efforts and sacrifice. Now that they had "made it" financially, it was time to say thank you the best way they knew how: with an Ed McMahon–style check.

Once again, the team of five met in their lounge in the back of the office and crafted a plan on how much they would distribute and when. It was important to all of them that their generosity be exactly what it was—a gift.

"They can cash their check and quit the next day," Mike said to the group. "I sure hope they don't, but it's got to be clear this is a token of appreciation. A *thanks for getting us here*. No strings attached."

The team set about identifying key employees they wanted to honor with the spoils of their deal. They came up with a total dollar amount they wanted to give out, and with Rebecca's help, they created a metric based on position and tenure.

The more they thought, the more names came to mind. In eleven short years, so many people had carried them.

In the end, they decided on fifty-five employees who would be receiving checks for various amounts. The secret could not get out, so the owners went about their day-to-day, saying nothing, hiding the strange smiles on their faces.

The distribution of cash to the "Core Fifty-Five" had to be epic. Worthy of Torchy's itself. They decided to send a formal invitation via email. The message was cryptic, almost like a Wonka ticket:

You're invited to a special event. The company would like to meet with you in downtown Austin at the following address…"

After it gave the location, date, and time, the message concluded with a simple request: *We ask that you keep this completely confidential.*

The night before they were set to meet, Mike was so excited he almost couldn't sleep. This was what he'd truly wanted all those years before. To provide opportunity. You only get this kind of joy in giving when you yourself have experienced want.

When you've stood in the Coinstar line with a jar of change, hoping it's enough to pay your light bill.

Or watched the late payment notices stack up on the kitchen table.

Or worked an after-school job while your friends played ball.

Or sat in your car with a phone in your hand, praying an order would come in and save your business.

The owners themselves had, at one point, felt all of this. The lifetime of struggling uphill. All of them had been in a place where they'd prayed for help. For the universe to cut them a freakin' break. For the owners, the generosity was not about tax deductions or good deeds even. It was an exercise in not forgetting where they'd come from. The hardships. The scrappiness that had become the secret to their alchemy.

When morning finally came, Rebecca, the resident stoic of the group, prepared her husband for the unexpected. "People don't always react to surprises in the way you might think," she said.

But truthfully, she had just as many butterflies as Farrell did. They'd written out personalized thank you notes, and she'd printed them at their house the night before so that she could be sure the paper was nice.

The meeting was held in downtown Austin at the Headliner's Club on the 21st floor of the Chase Tower. None of them were club members, but Farrell knew a guy who could get them in, and it seemed to go with the whole *Ocean's Eleven* vibe they were hoping for. "Best of all," Jay Wald said, "it has parking."

The room itself was basically a nice hotel ballroom with green velvet accents, but it had the mystique they were looking for, and it felt special. Again, as though magnets, the owners naturally arranged themselves in the same shape—a circle. There was no table with a head or a foot, just five high-back chairs and a sixth one that was empty.

"Hey, guys, there's Mike at age 70," Jay punched Mike on the arm. On the wall behind them was an oil portrait of an old guy smoking a cigar.

They didn't have time to laugh before the first employee came in, and they began what Farrell would later call, "the best day of my life, aside from my wedding and the birth of my kids."

For the nervous employees outside the heavy door, it was impossible to know what to expect. Most of them didn't think that they personally were in trouble, but was the company?

Has Torchy's been bought out? Is there some legal reason why the details of the meeting couldn't be shared?

One by one, the Torchy's team members came through the door. Nervous laughter and sweaty palms as they sat down in the sixth chair.

"Everything's cool," Mike would begin. "We just want to talk to you. As you know, we've been growing and growing, and you've been working your butt off right along with us. You've done everything we've ever asked of you, so here…" He would then hand them the fat envelope.

The checks ranged from $20,000 to $185,000, and they came with a personalized note (on Rebecca's heavyweight paper) that articulated that employee's strengths and expressed the deep gratitude of the ownership team.

As Rebecca predicted, some of the employees didn't know how to react. Some were afraid to look at it, so they just nodded in thanks.

"Open it up," Mike nudged. "It's yours."

And once they saw the amount, tears flowed for everyone.

Rebecca dotted the corner of her eyes, trying to act like she wasn't going to cry. Farrell stood and paced, smiling like a father on Christmas Day. Jay and Mike snorted back sobs and Fonz smiled and shook hands.

The money was life-changing, and the outpouring of appreciation would echo in the owners' ears for a long time after that day.

You don't know what this means…my whole life is going to change.

I can pay off my mortgage.

I can buy a car.

I can pay my student loans.

I can help my mother with her medical bills.

I didn't expect this.

I can't take this.

This is way too much.

My God, thank you.

The team made sure the recipients felt the freedom of the gift. "We'd like you to stay with Torchy's. We need you onboard so that we can continue to be successful, but to be clear—this is yours for what you've already done."

The giveaway also had an added benefit. Hungry young managers and others who felt they'd found a company they could stick with for the long haul suddenly had capital to invest. Basically, the money they were given, they could put right back in.

What surprised all of the owners was the domino of selflessness. The pay-it-forward moments playing out before their eyes.

Bheto Gonzalez, a cook who'd come over with Mike from Lucy's Boatyard, was among them. Bheto, with his strong work ethic and cheerful attitude, had risen in the ranks, from cook all the way to new store manager. He was traveling around the region, helping open new stores when they'd asked him to come back to Austin for the secret event.

He opened the check and put his hand to his mouth, forcing back tears. "I can put my cousin through college with this."

After the second day of giveaways, Farrell and Rebecca came home and the kids stared at them. "What's wrong, mom?" their son asked, noticing the puffy eyes.

"Happy tears," she said.

Later as they climbed into bed, Rebecca blew her nose. "Thank goodness there's not a third day, because I couldn't do it again," she said to Farrell. "Hallmark-channel kind of sobs."

Farrell was still riding the adrenaline high and wanting to relive the whole thing. "Who was your favorite?" he asked.

The team had decided not to record anything, so they could just be in the moment. Those two days were theirs. Without a recording, there would only be the memory shrouded in mystery.

In the end, $4.5 million was distributed to the Torchy's crew. Mike saved the last check for Juan, his first employee who had sweated with him in the roach coach all those years before—now, his kitchen manager. "Here you go, amigo. We did it."

CHAPTER 17

From Founder to New CEO...Sort Of

So goes the leader, so goes the rest.

Austin, 2018. Andrew Crawford and his business partner Shaw Joseph wasted no time on their assignment. After the General Atlantic pitch meeting concluded and the screens with the faces of the global partners went to black, the charge from Mr. Ford reverberated across the polished boardroom table and echoed in Crawford's ears.

Find Torchy's new CEO. Now.

The mission was clear. They all agreed that Torchy's was a rocket ship. Now it was time to find the astronaut to pilot it. Crawford enlisted the services of a top headhunter and, in relatively short order, found an astronaut who had appeared to have flown highly successful missions to the far edges of the solar system, somebody known as "one of the best restaurant operators" in the country.

To their credit, the equity firm had experienced such success because they were willing to do the due diligence up front and make sure that everyone was in sync. After a few weeks of working together, the goals of the owners could be simply stated. Their ambition was to grow the business beyond Texas, Oklahoma, and Colorado. To take the brand nationwide—if not worldwide—and then maybe go public. While the owners were confident in their skill sets and instincts, they were also self-aware enough to know that they would not attract top CEO talent without an institutional investor like General Atlantic to vouch for them.

One of the biggest changes in business ownership comes when the founder, or in Torchy's case, a group of what amounted to five co-founders, realizes that what got them to where they are today won't get them where they need to go tomorrow. The realization gives rise to what Noam Wasserman called "the founder's dilemma," which involves the need to negotiate a trade-off between wealth and control, between building financial value and having control of decisions. It's not a question of *whether* to forge ahead—"you're either growing or you're dying," Mike always said—but who to bring on board to lead that charge.

If you want to go from 40 restaurants to 100 or 200...if you want to go from the moon to the outer rings of Saturn, you need to find someone who has made the journey before. Someone who has put together a successful team of C-Suiters, for example. Someone who has been associated with brands that became household names not just in Austin or Texas but in Nashville, Atlanta and Washington, D.C.

And maybe even Columbus, Ohio.

You need someone who can help you professionalize and, anathema to the five owners' ears as the words sounded, become a bit more corporate without losing your soul, which was tantamount to saying without losing your passion for the product and people who craved it.

That's a hard balance to strike and for several turbulent years, between 2018 and 2021, Torchy's sought to find that sweet spot between optimizing their systems and operations for rapid growth and staying true to its "damn good" identity.

Common sense tells us that change takes time, but time was one thing the wise heads at Torchy's felt they didn't have tons of to spend. So, they evolved on the fly and in real time. Aligning the team during the pivot in leadership was of the utmost importance. As each person joined, they proved, in their own way, to be the "missing piece." The new CEO knew that professionalizing operations and office culture across the entire organization would be key to their ability to scale the business. So, he wasted no time putting in place a chief people officer to lead the charge. Other C-Suiters followed.

While the term "HR" was stale, 2D, conjuring up mostly policies and procedures, the people officer was both spokesperson and cultural ambassador. A wearer of many hats, at different times, therapist, cheerleader, even supreme court judge.

When they talked about acquiring talent, Torchy's didn't stop looking for people who could wear more than one hat, but it did begin to put in place a more centralized approach to hiring which allowed them to better predict hiring needs. The system was based on the Predictive Index, which was basically a test that revealed what kind of person someone is, their strengths and weaknesses as they apply to the workplace. In a state-of-the-art organization such as Torchy's sought to become, the PI was used to hire and train people with complementary skill sets and workstyles. In other words, they didn't want clones; they wanted a good, healthy diversity of opinions and know-how.

Torchy's also wanted people who could get their jollies working within a corporate rather than franchise model. While a franchise model might have worked for other people, Torchy's was firmly committed to having leadership emanate from a central nerve center. The way they saw it, franchises created a misalignment of goals between the franchisor (brand owners) and franchisees. In a franchise system, the franchisees have a greater focus on what is best for their individual location, while the franchisors are focused on what is best for the overall brand.

Besides, if you wanted to export your culture far, far beyond the familiar territory of the Southwest, you had to find your story and stick to it—not tell a thousand different tales.

It made perfect sense. If you're going to lead an empire, your people must believe the mission so they can carry the banner with them to every new shore. No professional operation today operates without a kick-ass set of core values, so in looking at Torchy's gritty past and hopes for the future, the whole Torchy's team, in the field and at HQ, came up with an acronym, TORCH: tenacity, originality, respect, community and honor.

Here's how they broke it down:

Tenacity: That meant perseverance with a plan. There wasn't just one way of thinking about a problem, but 101 ways of thinking about it.

Originality: Be yourself. Own it. Celebrate your distinction.

Respect: Respect is a way of looking at people and a means of behavior.

Community: Take care of your team first, so that you can take care of the community.

Honor: Have integrity. Stick to what you say.

And in the end, "TORCH" wasn't just a play on words, but itself a *playbook* and symbol. It was their torch that reminded them to be a beacon of light in their industry. Particularly when it needed it most.

And no functional area of Torchy's was excluded from carrying the TORCH. The company even professionalized its legal, safety, and risk functions. And the more core value boxes your idea or initiative checked off, the better.

EVER SINCE THE EARLY days of Torchy's, when Mike used to bring tacos to the people on his motor scooter, the company had been pretty bold about its marketing. They weren't about to stop this. Just because you are getting bigger and more complex doesn't mean you can't continue to be hip and sexy, right? The whole point of Torchy's culture was that loyal customers could taste the lack of fear and savor the presence of fun exuded by the staff. Now the fun would have to be on a larger scale, along with everything else.

One of the first projects Torchy's revamped marketing team spearheaded was Operation Taco Drop, a surprise event for Austin's annual film and music festival, South by Southwest. Basically, the Torchy's taco drop was just as one might guess: 200 "Trailer Park" tacos attached to mini-parachutes and released from a six-story building.

The preparation was no small feat. The parachutes had to be imported from Australia and taco test flights conducted before the launch. The marketing team had assumed, and rightfully so, that when it came to raining tacos, it was better to ask forgiveness than permission.

The stunt was as epic as they'd hoped: the taco UFOs floated down to cheering festival goers below. Torchy's had done it again. Surprised and delighted the masses with an edgy stunt.

Too bad the city didn't think so. They slapped Torchy's with a misdemeanor charge (but that was eventually dropped). Word on the street was that a taco remained suspended in a tree for 15 months. The small fine paid was worth it for the memory.

From an operations standpoint, the changes to Torchy's modus operandi were, perhaps, less spectacular than a taco drop, but in some ways more profound and every bit as impactful. Prior to the era of professionalization, for example, Torchy's was used to getting their sales with *zero tools*. They were all muscle. This was a far cry from some of their larger competitors who could bring in a new franchisee and give them a manual that told them everything. Such a manual was systemized down to the minute, so operators just followed along. *When you hit this many transactions, you need to put these people in these places.* From an optimization standpoint, they had the precision of a bomb drop.

Torchy's had standardized their menu, but outside of food, they had nothing in the way of infrastructure. This needed to change, starting with better analytics.

"We need to start building out some FP&A capability around here," people recall one member of the team announcing in one meeting. Judging by the confused looks around the table, it was clear most of the team didn't even know of the word. "Fiscal planning and analysis," he nudged. It was as if someone had dropped him off on an island with a machete and he was going to hack his way through the data to create some sort of recognizable path. Challenging but exhilarating.

"Basically, it means getting data that we can take action on. It's the very first step in getting visibility into your business."

But each store was its own unicorn. When a member of the leadership would ask a simple question, something like, "How many managers does this store have?"

The response was always, "Well...it depends."

And if there was ever a problem with a particular unicorn, they did what you do when you're leading with tenacity—they threw whatever they had at it—money, time, energy. They drew from their own checkbooks. They made bad investment deals. They borrowed from Peter to pay Paul. The simple mantra: *just get it done.*

But Torchy's leadership team weren't the Goonies anymore. They were, perish the thought, college boys and girls now with big money and big investors, and in order to scale, they'd need to—for the first time in their damn good history—ask questions. And it was their job to pose those questions in hopes of streamlining resources and energy. *Why are we spending three times the normal amount on a building that we project will generate the same revenue as everywhere else?*

BETWEEN 2018 AND 2021, business was booming at Torchy's by many measures. The chain grew from 45 restaurants to 96 locations in Texas, Oklahoma, Colorado, Louisiana, Kansas, Tennessee, Arkansas, and Indiana, opening 26 units in 2020 and 2021 despite pandemic pressure. In March 2021, Torchy's reported 4,468 employees, 68.2 percent of which were people of color and 50.8 percent were female.

And in November 2020, the rumors around the industry were confirmed by the headlines that read, *Torchy's Tacos Sells $400 Million Stake in Company.*

But what might have seemed like a fairytale ending to the Torchy's tale contained another major turn in that great cycle of joy and grief that always seemed to underpin the Little Devil's whirlwind of growth. For there was a crack in the edifice that those on the inside could see—a fissure too foundational to ignore, too deep to work around.

Torchy's had begun to lose a little of its soul. This is not an uncommon occurrence in highly successful, fast-growing businesses like Torchy's. Like a ship, the bigger a business gets, the harder it becomes to turn, which explains why they tend to become more risk-averse than smaller and more agile organizations.

But losing your soul was never going to be a part of any deal Mike would accept, no matter how many dollar signs were attached. So when the CEO retired in 2021, there was only one man standing who could be capable of stepping back in, even if it was only on an "interim" basis, and putting things right again.

And that was Mike. And so would begin the re-education of a founder. But before that happened, Torchy's had to get through the biggest challenge of its queso-loving life.

CHAPTER 18

The Year that Changed Everything

You will not grow if you are afraid of change.

Austin, 2020. At the start of 2020, Torchy's was a changed and changing place, as Torchy's professionalization had introduced the Managing Partner program. This time-tested model was a huge part of Texas Roadhouse's success, and Torchy's leadership believed that it would produce the same results for Torchy's.

Basically, the partnership allowed single-unit operators to buy into the business, and in turn, the restaurant would pay managers seven percent of the operating profit plus base pay. At the time of the transition, it meant that Torchy's would have not just five owners working to keep the company "damn good," but 71 of them. That's 71 people getting up in the morning, motivated to think about the dynamics of the business. To share in the pride and the spoils. Those who could boast of decades of experience with this model had never seen this method fail.

There's an old saying that if a cord has many strands, it's not easily broken. The many strands of ownership—which, in theory, were problematic—had actually provided strength. But after the deal with General Atlantic and the successful convergence of the professional team, it was clear to the Kubenas that they were no longer commanding a scrappy startup from their boardroom kitchen. What they had done with their own blood, sweat, and tears for twelve straight years was a miracle in anyone's book. Torchy's kept its feisty nature, but now, in the company's best interest, the principles of world-class business had entered the mix.

The people who composed Torchy's origin story were also starting to glimpse the reality of a life after Torchy's. Fonz had actually been the first to see this. If you asked anyone on the ownership team what Fonz did best, they'd say, "Whatever you need him to do." As Torchy's popularity had grown, Fonz had become the default head of technology. Not because he was super qualified (though he had good computer skills) but simply because he was willing to step up to the plate. But once Torchy's had the right infrastructure in place, it was clear he could relinquish his responsibilities within the company but remain a loyal owner.

Farrell and Rebecca, too, would soon come to the same conclusion. As she cleaned out her office, Rebecca tearfully flipped through an old binder with the projections she'd used to get their first honest-to-goodness bank loan. With tears in her eyes, she turned the pages, as if it were a scrapbook. "Remember when…" she said to Farrell.

Though she would never take credit, Rebecca had (like all the others), been carrying more than her share of the weight. When the new CFO came in he had jokingly asked, "So basically Rebecca's job has been anything accounting-related, anything finance-related, anything purchasing-related, anything HR-related? Did I leave anything out?"

But for Rebecca, the massive workload hadn't felt like a burden. She'd loved Torchy's like a child. But the Little Devil had grown up, and it was ready for bigger things. They had to do what was best for it.

Farrell, too, felt it was time to move on. His unorthodox method of choosing locations had served them when there were dozens of stores, but what about when there were hundreds or even thousands of them? He'd left his mark, his very fingerprints glued to the wall. Even the smart kids at Harvard who used Torchy's as a case study for real estate success couldn't quite figure out Farrell's metrics. And that made him happy.

But before he stepped back from the company, Farrell got to have one full-circle moment. When it was time to hire his assistant, he tapped Darby Stogner, the daughter of real estate agent Gray Stogner, the guy who'd first gambled on Torchy's at Darby's request. Darby had finished school and was stepping out into real estate in Austin. "You helped me out big time once. Why don't you let me pay you back? Come work for me. If you're anything like your dad, you've got instincts in spades."

Darby worked with Farrell for over a year. As one of Farrell's last legacies, he and Darby proposed a list of new markets—all the way up to store 100. The list had been chosen carefully. Torchy's growing name recognition was encouraging, but they didn't let that delude them into thinking they were ready to go fully national. Though their methodology had relied heavily on Farrell's Jedi sense, from the get-go, they'd been conservative, moving from market to market slowly, without getting out over their skis. It kept things close: the culture, the people, the vendors. Instead of being lured by the big markets, they allowed the culture to grow organically, even if that meant putting in a Torchy's in Odessa, Texas, before they put one in New York or Chicago.

When it came to the topic of real estate, Torchy's brain trust had another goal that, in some ways, you could call a premonition. By early 2019, as food delivery platforms got off the ground, it occurred to some that younger customers had higher demands. They wanted to be in control of the when, where, and how they got their food.

You don't have to be a rocket scientist to see that Torchy's wasn't using all possible channels. At the time, Torchy's off-premise sales were not bad by industry standards, but their cash was definitely coming from dine-in guests. But the writing was definitely on the wall: people were more on-the-go than ever. They had to meet the guests where they were. That meant bolstering their carry-out and delivery.

"At least half of our sales should be off premise," was the word circulating through headquarters.

"Half is a pretty big jump," Mike thought.

It was definitely a shift in thinking. The brick-and-mortar Torchy's stores were crushing it, so naturally, the company had planned to keep its head down and stay the course. Focus on opening more restaurants. Making them bigger and better.

But Mike had never been one to reject an idea simply because it was different, so Torchy's began implementing ways to make food mobile. In an effort to ensure the best off-site dining experience possible, they focused on to-go packaging. In January 2019, they launched a run of catering and party packs. They also pushed their limited game-day menu. (This was particularly exciting for Cheryl, who, as a culinary perfectionist, had long been advocating for streamlining their offerings so that execution could be flawless every time.) In March of that same year, the team landed an exclusive partnership with DoorDash, the largest and fastest-growing on-demand vehicle for door-to-door deliveries. By the end of the year, the Torchy's team, without realizing it, had laid the foundation that was going to save them.

"I KNOW IT'S A Saturday, but I think you need to come over to my house." Torchy's top people-person paced in her kitchen. On the phone, the last person she needed to reach to assemble Torchy's "Emergency Team."

The news had been buzzing for over a week. A deadly virus was making its way across the globe. On every channel, the same words scrolled across the bottom of the screen, words she'd never heard used in her lifetime, words like *outbreak* and *pandemic*.

Still, it seemed everyone around her was going about business as usual. It didn't make sense. Maybe she'd spent too much time focusing on disasters, but the whole thing left her with a pit in her stomach, as if they were trapped in an end-of-the-world box office thriller and no one was batting an eye.

"This thing is here," she said once the Emergency Team had gathered in her living room. "It isn't going away any time soon, and that means we've got to get ahead of it."

For the next several hours, the team set themselves the task of asking some hard questions.

How do we deal with the sick?

How do we respond to guests?

How do we ensure cleanliness?

How do we make sure we get PPE equipment?

They went down the rabbit trails of "what-ifs," and at the end of an exhausting weekend, what they had was a sort of operations manual. A worst-case-scenario guide in the event that everyone around them was wrong and they were right.

Thankfully, the people team was already hard at work in refining the culture of headquarters. Torchy's had always prioritized its guests, no question, but it had always lived by the motto, "Our stores are our first customers, and we need to put them first." It was a simple trickle-down effect. Everything started with the individual stores feeling supported. *Take care of the stores, and they will take care of the guests.* The year 2020 would put that theory to the test.

Once things got worse, once faces were masked and *coronavirus* was on everyone's lips, the leadership team had to face up to the dreaded "F" word.

"Torchy's was either going to have to start furloughing...or get *really* creative," was the directive delivered to the people team leader.

"Give me the weekend," she said, grabbing her coffee and throwing her car keys in her bag.

Again, she holed up in her house to sort things out. Her goal: figure out how to keep everyone at headquarters.

It was like a giant sudoku with people's lives, but after 48 hours of thinking, she had a plan. She convinced a few members to take lesser pay, and only had to furlough six people from HQ. "And the six we furloughed I think we can bring back quickly, if we shift them into slightly different roles," she told the leadership team.

Given this leeway to take care of Torchy's team didn't mean there weren't hard decisions to make. At COVID's peak, the company was forced to temporarily close a handful of stores in areas most affected by the pandemic.

But they followed the plan. They focused on supporting their own first, continuing to pay benefits and insurance for those on furlough and offering free COVID testing to employees. They kept furloughed employees in the loop on company news, ensuring they still felt part of the Torchy's community.

The crisis would show the Torchy's team just what it was made of. Individual locations created makeshift curbside pickups; they set up tents and moved their point-of-sale system outdoors. A few of them even rigged up drive-thru windows.

Change is hard, but in the restaurant industry, as in any business, you must adapt or die. At the beginning of the pandemic, the team was planning to open 20 new restaurants, but in a matter of weeks, they, like everyone else, had dropped to 100 percent off-premise sales. Torchy's secured a loan through the Paycheck Protection Program (which was paid back in full), and thanks to some quick, innovative thinking, by August 2020, the company brought back 1,400 furloughed employees. Though they had to alter their growth plan, they opened 12 new stores in three new states (Missouri, Louisiana, and Kansas). In 2020, they were even able to hire 1,000 new team members to support their expansion. On opening day at each location, the taco junkies (with masks on) lined up around the block.

The cherry on top was the launch of new products at other retailers. In February 2020, Torchy's Green Chile Queso and full-flavored spicy Diablo Sauce hit the shelves of approximately 40 Whole Foods in states within their market. Even with a slow roll out, having bottles of queso and sauce on supermarket shelves clearly showed the power of the brand. The reception proved the products were a wanted commodity. The queso had legs. The sky was the limit.

For this unlikely success through COVID, Mike had to tip his hat to resilience, preparedness, and per usual, a little providence. More than ever, he was thankful for the partnerships. As Torchy's would tell the media, which was intrigued by their success, "We stuck with our current landlords, we paid our vendors. A lot of other companies haven't been able to pivot as much as we have."

But frankly, the ride was scary as hell.

Mike had his own reflection of the year. In some ways, he considered 2020 a gift. It was a return to his roots. A reminder of the kind of grit that's not fostered in business school but in the fires of hardship.

"It brought us back to what made us successful in the first place," Mike said. "Tenacity. And just trying to figure out creative ways to get the food to the people again."

CHAPTER 19

High Stakes

Hardships are the time to go on the offensive.

Austin, 2020. Jay Sonner was back in the Torchy's saddle again. Just four short years before, Jay had been getting to know North Point's hippest newest client in the penthouse of the Andaz Hotel in West Hollywood. Assessing the wants and needs of a company is sometimes drudgery, but the team's work-hard-play-hard mentality was refreshing, and the owners loved each other as fiercely as they loved their jobs. Jay had a sense about them: Torchy's wasn't just a hot brand. It was here for the long haul.

Fast forward to the fall of 2020, and Jay's feelings about the company back in LA in 2017 had been borne out ten-fold. In a year of unprecedented turmoil for the restaurant industry, the spark that was Torchy's was still bright, and it shone even more so against the dark backdrop of the pandemic. At a time when many companies were defaulting on leases and taking down marquees, Torchy's was still killing it. With the help of General Atlantic, the next layer of sophistication—the professional team—had been well established. Torchy's had 83 units in 10 states and an average unit volume (AUV) of 3.8 million in 2019. In short, the restaurant space was the world of haves and have-nots.

And Torchy's was the haves.

Seeing hardship in the market as an opportunity to go on the offensive, the Torchy's leadership team decided it was time to consider a second round of fundraising, so they reached out to North Point again to help guide them through another equity deal. Jay Sonner had barely put the feelers out, and suddenly the big players in the investment world were climbing all over each other to get a piece of the opportunity. Like moths to the queso flame.

Jay was making the long, scenic drive home along California's State Route 1 when one of the first calls with a global investment group took place. At this point in his career, Jay had listened in on this kind of deal a thousand times before. It was the job. What he did all day— every day. But this call was special. Jay had spent plenty of time with Torchy's leadership team, but he'd never heard a presentation as frankly spellbinding as the one he heard that day. As close as you can get in the investment world to an *aria*. Jay knew all there was to know about Torchy's, and yet he was hanging on the Torchy's people's every word. Somewhere between San Luis Obispo and Carmel-by-the-Sea, Jay pulled his car over so he wouldn't lose cell service.

Torchy's top brass had given the spiel before, only this time they were aware that the people on the listening end represented over a trillion dollars of investments.

So they lit it up.

"There is a massive hole in the supply of an experience like Torchy's in relation to the consumer demand," they began. "If you go to Houston, there are twenty-something Torchy's and maybe three Shake Shacks. Why is that? The restaurants have very similar models. They both have great buildouts. They're modern and polished. But here's the difference: the burger market is saturated. Shake Shack is playing in a crowded space. Think about Manhattan—how many Torchy's could you put there? A crap-ton! There's nothing going head-to-head with it. It's unique enough that if there are a hundred stores in the next year, there could eventually be a thousand."

Jay was staring through his windshield at the white-capping Pacific when North Point's big boss made his closing remarks.

"Well," the big boss said. "I'd love the opportunity to get in with you again before you even have a story."

There was a pause.

Jay Sonner knew what the big boss meant. The potential for Torchy's to go public was real. The parties who were private-public market agnostic (meaning they liked to invest in both private and public businesses) were clamoring for the opportunity to get involved *before* a company went public. Getting into something before the secret was out was like finding gold. What made the prospect even more enticing was the fact that a big U.S. restaurant hadn't gone public in almost six years. Of course, there had been restaurant hopefuls who had professionalized management and garnered some interest, but they petered out before they made it across the finish line. They started focusing on the nickels and dimes and, somewhere along the way, they lost the essence of what got them there in the first place.

The prospect was exciting. Would the Little Devil, this ugly duckling of a taco joint, potentially break what would be a six-year dry spell for large restaurant chains in the public market?

Time would tell.

At the close of the call, one thing was clear to everyone involved—the train was leaving the station, and investors wanted on for the ride.

TORCHY'S WASN'T JUST GROWING its market during the pandemic, it was growing its team. For anyone, it was a risky time to be venturing out into a new field, particularly one that had been as devastated as the hospitality industry. By December 2020, 10,000 restaurants in Texas had reportedly shut down, and 110,000 restaurants across the nation had closed. But as one new Torchy's manager said, "You can brave an unknown sea if the vessel and captain are sound."

Which is exactly how, during a global pandemic, a second round of professional players left their successful jobs to join what was, on paper, a regional taco company.

When it comes to IT, companies tend to fall roughly into two camps, with plenty of room on the spectrum to accommodate exceptions. One camp consists of companies that hire technology wonks, trusting that somebody on the business side speaks techno well enough to communicate with colleagues in IT. The other camp wants somebody who possesses the strengths of the typical IT guy—efficient, good problem solver—but who also has a strong penchant for business. Torchy's fell squarely into the second camp.

"There's no point in implementing technology if you don't understand the business," was the school of thought Mike and those on the business side used to argue. "Guests aren't going to wait for you to innovate."

Simple enough, but many CTOs were missing it. Creating tech for tech's sake. Recognizing that the future of growth was all visual—the website, mobile app—all of it intended to ensure the guest has the best experience possible. Torchy's needed an IT team who could build a service-first, best-in-class department to support operations and propel growth in the next phase.

And they got one, right in the middle of a pandemic.

The challenges of running IT for Torchy's were apparent from the start. From a technology standpoint, it was basically a fifteen-year-old start-up. Scaling a company that is already doing a Torchy's-sized volume of business would be like building a freeway while cars are speeding down it. Since they couldn't shut down the freeway, they'd have to stabilize what was already in place, making the necessary structural changes while the company was running at a hundred miles an hour. Next, they would need to standardize all technology offerings and build out business processes within them. All of this while staying on the cutting edge of innovation: curbside check-in, online ordering, the list would go on and on. Accounting systems, cost systems, HR systems, finance systems. IT, like HR, was a department that supported every other department within the company. But if HR was the heart of the company, IT was its bones.

It was a tall order, but one Torchy's would have to fill. The IT "upgrade" is still a work in progress at Torchy's; anybody there would tell you that. But they have already upped their game in significant ways, not least of which was implementing enterprise accounting platforms that allow the company to run the company and scale with far greater ease.

Even as Torchy's was standardizing its processes, it never quite abandoned its old jack-of-all-trades mentality of encouraging synergies wherever possible, and especially between departments that in other companies would each have played in its own sandbox. Such was the case with bus dev, real estate, and supply chain.

In looking at the supply side, for example, the name of the game was scalability. To get Torchy's to grow outside the contiguous states of Texas, they had to find a way, as their supply chain champion put it, "To get the right product, in the right place, at the right time, and at the right cost." This meant focusing on relationships with distribution partners so that Torchy's could bring in the suppliers it needed. The suppliers would honor Torchy's unique flavors by prioritizing proprietary products. Quality would remain paramount.

From a real estate standpoint, the pandemic had turned the faucets off for most of 2020. But going into 2021, the team was cautiously optimistic, shifting the focus to meet the needs of guests in the post-COVID age: locations with more patio seating and less square footage (3,800 to 4,800 square feet). It was expensive to wait until after operations had been handed the keys to put in change orders for a particular store, so the folks at "corporate" suggested that they start involving Market Partners as soon as they'd identified the new space. They'd keep the uniqueness of their locations. Each store could be a snowflake, but they'd be more consistent where they needed to, e.g., standardizing the kitchen layout and other behind-the-scenes spaces.

The team had a goal to open 17 more stores, the 100th location among them. Despite all the odds, the growth from regional to super-regional to nationwide was still in sight.

CHAPTER 20

The Next Generation

In the end, it's STILL about the culture.

Austin, 2021. The culture that started in Bill's driveway (when the power chord was axed) was unlike any other in the restaurant space. The new team knew this. They promised to remember it, preserving it for the next generation, even as they grew exponentially. With the help of their People Team leader they set about implementing ways to keep the culture intact.

They would keep culture intact by caring for their own.

In the old days, the owners took turns paying their mortgages. They gave the tip jar to the busboy when his car had a flat. They paid the burial costs for a prep cook who had an unexpected death in the family.

They did these things without thinking. No questions asked. The no-man-left-behind attitude was never relegated to the dining room floor during lunch rush. It was in the after-hours and in the hospital waiting rooms.

The culture of giving had been imprinted on Torchy's since the beginning, so as the team grew, the leadership team had an idea of how to take that spirit into the next generation: the Torchy's Family Foundation. It would be led by the C-suite and completely internally funded. There were no barriers to entry for teammates in need. No insurance-like waiting periods before you could apply. Requests would be responded to within 48 hours.

Torchy's was already helping its people. This was just a way to organize it. In 2021, with thousands of employees, they might not have been taking money from the cash register anymore, but they were still promising to be each other's safety nets. More employees meant more need. But it also meant more hands to help.

The motorcycle accident. The long-term caretaker of an aging parent. The home ravaged by fire or flood.

"Sometimes you have to give it all away so you can give it back to the people who matter most," Mike once said at a meeting with the People Department. The quote stuck. That would be the motto of the foundation. She had the T-shirts printed to prove it.

In March 2021, Mike and the C-suite together pledged to give money to the Torchy's Family Foundation over the course of its first five years.

They would preserve their culture by acknowledging and elevating their people.

There are plenty of ways for a company to honor its employees, but at Torchy's, it's going to be fun.

One way to underpin culture is to listen to the people who are creating it. Since his earliest days in the industry, Mike had known who really made the money for the restaurants—the front lines. This was his secret. His reason for holding "town halls," which the new generation of Torchy's would call Damn Good Days.

There was also the Torchy's annual Conference. An actual stage is brought in to recognize people. The yearly, four-day event is known in the Torchy's world as "epic." The contagion of tent revival, the cool of Woodstock, the camaraderie of summer camp. (The giveaways have included a $25,000 check and a new Range Rover.)

But it's the recognition of character that seems to have the most lasting impact. At the event in 2020, the leadership team gave out the first ever "Legacy Award." While most of the honors at Torchy's are peer led, this one was not nomination-based. It was chosen by Mike himself.

"And the winner is Jay Wald—of course."

It was a simple choice, really. Jay was there in the beginning, back when the walk-in cooler was still duct taped to the wall. He was the guy who, at the El Paso store, once jammed his own hand into the floor to clear a clogged grease trap.

Everyone around him knew his level of hard work and commitment—and sacrifice. He'd put his body in front of a moving train to help a server in the weeds. He was the mainstay of operations and the heartbeat of innovation through all of Torchy's change. It was only fitting that Jay Wald was the first recipient of the Legacy Award. His hard work set the bar.

A final and perhaps most thrilling means of acknowledging their own was with Damn Good Culture. This immersion experience was, in the People Team leader's words, "Orientation 3.0."

Yes, a person would be hired for a particular role within Torchy's, but COVID had left its mark on the hiring process. They needed team members to be more flexible, so that, if necessary, they could shift roles within the company. They hoped to find individuals who were more committed to the brand than the title.

The quarterly bus tour of Torchy's history was one way to encourage that. It was the embodiment of *show, tell, do*, taking their people to former locations, the ghosts of Torchy's past and future. Pre-COVID, the team had tested the concept with managing and market partners and have plans to offer it to every level of the company down the road.

On the tour, Mike would emcee. The starting point, the self-proclaimed "South Austin Trailer Park and Eatery," by the banks of Bouldin Creek, under the shady oaks where critic Alison Cook first fell in love with the "Trailer Park" taco.

From there, maybe they would stop off at the gas-station-turned-commissary, and Jay could talk about the elements of the first supply chain: Walmart Tupperware and a delivery van.

Maybe then they would go to Headquarters and talk with Andy about the future of tech. Then drop off at the test kitchen east of Austin in Manor, Texas. There, they could see Cheryl in her native habitat, testing out cheese and chilis. They would check out the Torchy's relics: old menu boards, iron murals, even the taco cannon.

So many stories. So many quirky mementos that held a key to their past. The points of light that added up to who they were today.

The tour would end with a fireside chat, with Mike and other leaders discussing what they had learned from the past. What they hoped for the future.

"Wouldn't it be cool if we could make a Torchy's Duck Boat tour?" Mike joked. "Drive the damn thing into Lake Austin and see the sights that way?"

Their team culture would be as unique and diverse as the flavors they represented.

Not only did 2020 present the challenge of COVID-19, but it was also a call to awakening. The Black Lives Matter movement was shining a light on diversity and inclusion.

While the movement was gaining much-needed attention around the country, this was something that had been on Mike's heart since the beginning. "We've always loved our people of every kind. Every skin tone. Torchy's would have never gotten through its first week without the support of some of my friends in the Latino community."

With help from the People Team, Torchy's also started Damn Good Women. Recognizing that women in the restaurant business are drastically underrepresented, especially in leadership, Torchy's wanted to encourage their growth. So Damn Good Women was born. The quarterly event brings in outside speakers and covers topics relevant to women out in the field—from the line cooks to the leadership—in an effort to support female teammates as they take on more responsibilities and bigger roles.

A company should constantly take stock. See where it can do more to elevate diversity and inclusion, but this blueprint came naturally because it was woven into Torchy's very DNA. Torchy's very first people came from two lone criteria: *Can you be kind to people, and can you work?*

Yes? Great! Everything else is irrelevant.

In March 2021, Torchy's reported 4,468 employees, 68.2 percent of which were people of color and 50.8 percent were female.

They preserve culture by honoring their heritage.

One way to remember their legacy was to dip back into the pool of irreverence. To keep taco fans guessing. Maybe even surprise them.

The team acknowledged that this is hard to do during a pandemic. The most important thing is keeping customers safe while they satisfied their craving. COVID would put parameters on everything, but slowly, as the new normal set in, the Torchy's team felt it was okay to daydream again. Keep people on their toes.

"Okay," the head of marketing addressed his think tank, "we haven't done something crazy in a while."

And the 2020 presidential election would provide the perfect opportunity. At a time when every other business was running from anything that could be construed as political, the Torchy's team ran straight towards it. Using their Democrat and Republican tacos, they poked fun at both sides. They ran fake attack ads. As the marketing head said, "We're going to be an equal opportunity offender."

They made T-shirts, buttons, and banners boasting their presidential pair.

Taco Queso 2020.

Who could argue with that?

"HERE'S THE HEADLINE," JAY Sonner said in his signature tone that was a mix between a sports announcer and a court litigator. "An investor pulled out."

He was talking about the equity deal. They had been giving speeches and wooing investors for months, and now it was time to lock it down. Though Jay dropped the news matter-of-factly, Mike and the rest of the gang couldn't help but catch their breath. Everything had been going well. But these things were always tentative, weren't they? One puff of wind and the house of cards was in danger of collapse.

The investor was a big one, and their withdrawal was in the final countdown.

"But don't worry," Jay told them, "Basically, it's not going to be a thing."

As the team understood it, the investor was out on a technicality. When an investment company got that big, the people were no longer the decision-makers. Essentially, the legal team was tripping over each other to follow the letter of the law.

Despite the thirty-six hours of chaos that ensued, Jay was right. The loss of the enormous investor turned out to be no great loss at all. The situation was—as they say in Jay Sonner's world—"oversubscribed." In layman's terms, that meant that Torchy's was the prettiest girl at prom. If one suitor dropped out, there were ten more waiting to dance.

After the hot pursuit, in November 2020, it was official. The headlines were everywhere.

Torchy's Tacos Sells $400 Million Stake in Company.

General Atlantic, the global growth equity group that had initially invested in Torchy's in 2017, would be joined by new investors: D1 Capital Partners, T. Rowe Price, Lone Pine Capital, and XN.

The company that Mike and Juan had been running in a tin can, in the August heat, had just received not only affirmation but significant funding from some of the world's most sophisticated investors.

"Well," Sonner laughed in delight. "Once again, this valuation was the highest restaurant valuation I'm aware of. It was a high watermark three years ago, and it's a high watermark again—even in a pandemic."

The Torchy's team couldn't have been happier. GA, their solid partner for over three years, would have a majority stake, and Andrew Crawford, who'd been their comrade since Farrell was making cold calls, would become the new Torchy's chairman.

Pairing General Atlantic with four giants of investing was exactly what Torchy's needed to stay in the *growth zone*, which translated to putting Torchy's in 10 new states in the next four years.

Not only would the team create more locations, they pledged to cut the wait in existing stores, projecting they could get lunch ticket times from 12 to 15 minutes down to just 7 to 9. The competitor inside the beating heart of every Torchy's trooper knew there was never time to rest. They had to keep pushing or else the next guy would come in and eat their lunch. Literally.

The Original Five might have gone their separate ways, but during the second equity deal, something pretty special happened.

Instead of taking their winnings and walking away, all five founders put money back in. They believed in this thing back when it was a trailer, and they believe in it still.

CHAPTER 21

Back to the Beginning

People don't work for corporations; they work for people.

New York City, 2021: In mid-March 2021, word leaked on Wall Street that the stars were aligning for Torchy's to make the big move and go public. Though the headline on MarketScreener ended with a question mark—*Morgan Stanley: Torchy's Tacos looking at $1B IPO?*— the message seemed definitive. According to Bloomberg, General Atlantic had chosen Morgan Stanley, Bank of America, and JP Morgan Chase to handle the IPO, and it felt like the clock was ticking toward the moment Mike Rypka had always dreamed of. But back in Austin, the leadership team knew the news was premature.

While the company had added a dozen new stores in 2020, the COVID challenges had begun to impact the wild per-store numbers that had pushed the value of the company so high. As spring turned to summer and the IPO wasn't filed, it became obvious that the wisdom was to tap the brakes on going public. There were several reasons for the hesitation.

First, with the retirement of its CEO, Torchy's needed a new leader who would be around for a while to lead it into whatever future awaited it. Second, the twin engines of COVID and rapid growth had thrown Torchy's culture out of whack enough that the present needed some serious tending before the future could become clear.

"We were basically adjusting to a whole new normal," Mike said. "None of us knew what that was going to look like and the thought was we need to go head-down and work our way through to whatever it was going to look like."

THE GENERAL ATLANTIC TEAM didn't have to look far to find the retired CEO's replacement. After four years in a more supportive role working alongside the old leadership team, Mike was back! As the man that built the culture, who designed the menu, who breathed life into that original trailer, he was the perfect fit and was immediately named interim CEO.

"They asked me to interview the candidates for the CEO job," Mike recalled. "I interviewed them, and a couple of them were pretty good fits, but as I listened to them I realized I wanted to do it. I wanted to come back into the frying pan, high sizzle. Stepping away as CEO gave me the space I needed to decompress, spend time with my son

Michael, and see the company from a new vantage point. But you know what? I didn't realize how much I missed the pressure and the energy! COVID provided some real challenges, but I have to say I'm excited by trying to help find solutions."

The brass at GA agreed and gave Mike the green light to go back to the beginning and grab the reins and see whether he could steer that child of his through adolescence into full-blown adulthood.

Almost the first thing Mike did as *CEO redux* was hit the road to touch base with the people who are so integral to everything Torchy's was and will be. He wanted to tap into the old energy but also to take the pulse of the growing family restaurants. "Our managing partner program is such an important part of how we've grown and how that will continue," Mike said, adding, "and I am enjoying the opportunity to get back in front of those partners and ask how we solve any issues they're seeing. I'm re-energized and my passion is as strong as it was the day we opened the food truck!"

The managing partner program operated by putting one partner in charge of six to 12 Torchy's. Each partner reported up through operations at HQ, a structure that was meant to ensure the cascading out of Torchy's culture and business strategy.

"There's been some fun new energy that we can feel out there with our teams with that 'the original guy is back' narrative," Mike said. "But I'm also enjoying getting into the details. The Devil's in the details in business and I've loved coming back in and asking "why" we're doing some things today. I believe those are always healthy discussions."

You don't want to ask *why* if you're afraid of the answer you'll receive, so when Mike's tour took him into a Torchy's in Dallas or Houston or wherever, he had heard rumors that staff in many locations were completely stressed out and miserable. If he was going to get to the bottom of why this might be the case, he would need straight-shooting all-around.

And that's pretty much what he got.

The main problem was understaffing. A well-run Torchy's requires at least three managers: one to run the kitchen, one to run the service and the general manager to run the whole show. But the imperative to open new stores at a rapid pace often meant opening to the public before adequate staffing was in place. The result was bad both inside Torchy's four walls and outside.

Recalled Mike, "Everyone was working too many shifts with no time off. As a result, service suffered, the cuisine suffered, and our hospitality scores and guest scores on line and on premise suffered. As for the staff, especially the managers, the lack of manpower meant that when anyone called in sick the rest of the staff were "totally screwed." Managers were going too long without a day off. "Some of them were close to tears," Mike said.

One manager, whom Mike met during his travels to reacquaint himself with Torchy's, actually did cry, right in front of her staff and the founder, himself. The image of those tears stayed with Mike on the return trip to Austin. And they stayed with him after he pulled into the house, threw his carryon on the bed, and walked into the glass-encased humidor nestled in the corner of the living room. Selecting a 1964 Anniversary Series #4 cigar, he walked back through the living room and stood on the little deck overlooking a small wooded lot. And he came to some decisions.

Life's too short to be miserable, thought Mike, thinking back to the image of the unhappy manager. It didn't take into consideration that this kind of thing hadn't exactly happened on his watch. Torchy's was still his baby, so he felt accountable. On the one hand, reflected Mike, sending a plume of rich Nicaraguan-grown tobacco smoke into the moonlit darkness, we have chosen to make things a little harder for ourselves. We run kitchens that make things from scratch—"places with knives and fire," in Ryan Moore's words—as opposed to bags of frozen stuff made elsewhere.

Running a scratch kitchen is a challenge, so let's make sure we get these stores properly staffed, and let's make sure that as we grow and add new teammates, that our new employees have a damn good first day and embrace the culture. Of course, that assumes that the culture is there to embrace.

And then the outline for his second tenure in charge of Torchy's began to shape, a *Back to the Future* tableau that involved getting back to the basics. How many times had Mike said, "People may start a job because of pay, but they stay at a job because of culture?" A lot. "Let's focus on running great shifts, serving damn good tacos, and having damn good service. It's real simple. We don't have to complicate it past that," he thought.

By the time Mike finished his Padron, the evening had cooled and Mike had worked out, at least in his head, the basis of the Winning Formula.

"I THINK WE'RE READY to take this thing to the moon!" Mike told his operations leader, Jay Wald, and finance guru Ryan Moore, when the three men found themselves back at HQ nursing a cup of coffee. "Let's have some fun again. Let's take some risks and put the magic of Torchy's back into the company," he told them.

Mike's pronouncement was like an elixir in Jay and Ryan's ears. They had to admit that Torchy's had lost its way as the company spread from state to state. For example, as the marketing department grew and grew, it added more and more initiatives that strayed further and further away from basic good service.

"It got to the point that the person taking orders out front had to run through so many first-time customer promotions every time someone walked in the door, they forgot the basic stuff, like greeting the customer," Mike recalled. "Overall, it was business school marketing stuff and customer retention orthodoxy, which is fine but not at the expense of actually *taking care of people*, which is what is meant by hospitality."

The era of simplification, as Jay called the period beginning in 2021, wasn't about putting the brakes on growth. It was about re-establishing the fundamentals that served as a platform for growth.

"If you don't have a great pace and good fundamentals, trying to introduce more complex tools or scenarios is going to be really difficult," Jay explained, drawing on an analogy near and dear to his heart. "It's kind of like a football team. You want to have guys running more complex patterns and making more advanced plays, but before you can do that you have to master blocking, tackling, footwork, and so on. It's the same way for operations."

Once you've got your Winning Formula in place, you have your mission and marching orders all wrapped up in a little bow. For example, you know the kinds of people you want to hire don't necessarily need to have worked in large chains, but they do need to "exude hospitality and an obvious enjoyment in being in the public eye and talking to people," in Mike's words. Somebody who can work in a high-volume, fast-paced kitchen and execute on a schedule.

"We're a heavy people business, so we have to lead with compassion and empathy," noted Jay. "Our jobs as leaders, vice presidents, chiefs, all that kind of stuff, is to remove complexity from the operators so they can serve our guests better. So we better be making sure we take as much heavy lifting off them as we can so that they can focus on the important things."

But the truth is that while the current Era of Simplification at Torchy's may be built on culture, scaling that culture to become 150 locations, the company's short-term goal, requires plenty of technology and marketing horsepower as well. That's why it pays to have partners like GA who not only share your vision but also have deep pockets to invest in the goodies you need to grow big and strong.

One of those goodies was dubbed Project Blue Sky, which involved working with outside consultants to audit Torchy's restaurant operations and recommend ways to become more efficient in how the restaurant ran its kitchen, managed its supply chain, and interacted with guests. They toured restaurants, interviewed guests, pored through everything from the marketing materials to the recipe book, and produced a host of great ideas, many of which have been, or are being, fully operationalized.

"The consultants talked about some of the ways we could change our back-of-the-house processes and products, while still remaining a scratch kitchen, which is a big differentiator for us," said Jay.

One of the recommendations involved pushing some of the food prep to the supplier, a common practice that would ease on-premise preparation without compromising freshness and made-to-order dishes. Another recommendation involved food engineering to achieve greater scale out of each menu item.

Jay explained it this way: "If I make green chili pork that goes in one pocket of the green chili pork taco, and I also make barbacoa that goes into the Democrat taco, I have created twice the work. Each taco requires a different workstation, and together they are time consuming to produce. But if I can take a recipe of pork as the base, I can add three or four different toppings and make four different kinds of pork tacos."

Not only less upfront work, but also less opportunity for food wastage, the perpetual scourge of restaurant operators the world over.

Another innovation that is proving near and dear to an old food truck chef's heart is the smart oven. With the push of a button, a chef can "set it and forget," as Mike said. "Smart ovens allow us to have fewer cooks in the kitchen bumping into each other with pots and pans. When you're a small company, the cook makes a thousand little determinations for every dish. You're constantly messing with the flame and stirring. With a smart oven, you could just literally put the dish inside, hit the cow button, and walk away to do something else. And it cooks your beef and beeps when the dish is done to specification. Best of all, the harmonious flavors and texture you're looking for are identical to what you get cooking on a stovetop."

On the business side, one of the technology upgrades Jay says has "revolutionized us" is called Domo, a reporting tool that allows businesses to collect data on every aspect of the restaurant and run just about any report imaginable. "This has been a big collaboration between our technology and finance teams," he noted.

"Do you want to see which of the Torchy's stores is making the best use of Uber Eats on a monthly basis? Domo will break down sales and average order price for whatever region or area code you designate. Or, do you want to get a sense of the ideal number of employees needed for each location that uses smart oven technology? Domo will break down your kitchen process by work hours and give you that number.

"As we expand, we're creating labor models to try to get our stores to efficiency as we're rolling out a new kitchen process," said Mike. "So we need to know what *good* looks like. These models are very intuitive and use algorithms to project out by transactions, how many hours a week they should be running on their schedule. These are allowing us to project hiring 65 people rather than 85 as we open new stores."

Marketing was a sore spot at Torchy's in the years leading up to the Era of Simplicity. Too many marketeers running too many campaigns that produced too few results worth measuring. "It was even decided to drop the word "Tacos" from Torchy's in emerging markets," Mike huffed. "You don't drop the name of your product unless you're a household name like Dunkin' Donuts with tens of thousands of locations. At one point, someone actually thought Torchy's was the name of a brothel."

With Domo, the new and greatly streamlined marketing team could go out and do "scrapes" of all Torchy's Google, Facebook and Yelp reviews from a digital side, collate these with the on-premise surveys that were collected and get an overall guest satisfaction score for each individual store.

Turning a successful regional brand into a successful national brand takes a fine balance of urgency and patience. It begins with earning loyalty until eating your food becomes a habit, and then understanding how that habit travels with the customer.

"I tell our team this all the time," said Mike. "How many restaurants do you pass every week without giving them a second thought? A lot, right? And it's not like they have a sign out front that says, "We suck. Don't come in because we have rats in the kitchen and our service sucks. They don't come in because they just don't know who you are. People are creatures of habit, so you have to give them reasons to return so that when they're driving through a new city or past a big strip mall in a new community, they see your restaurant and remember the free queso and salsa they enjoyed a few weeks ago and stop at your store."

As Torchy's makes its national trek East, West, and North from Texas through America's heartland and pushes into new frontiers in places like Columbus, Ohio, Atlanta, Georgia, and Washington D.C., it will continue to pave the way with grand openings and Taco of the Month specials and free queso and salsa for anyone who feels the draw from the little devil in the diaper.

"We're just going to keep on telling people who we are and keep on opening new restaurants and improving our operations," offered Mike by way of summary. "And do them all at the same time."

DURING THE CRAZY MONTHS when Mike made the decision to return as Torchy's CEO and throw himself back into fire, Mike knew there was one conversation he absolutely had to have. It wasn't with a trusted colleague or investment partner. It was with his son. For the past four years, Mike's now 11-year old son Michael had been a regular companion. They had been able to enjoy the father-son time that isn't always a part of the day-to-day life of an entrepreneur, especially one in the restaurant world. It was time that Mike The Torchy's Builder didn't get for the first seven years of Michael's life. But during that window, they had gone to events and openings of Torchy's stores where Michael had been able to sit with his father and marvel at the crowds. Prior to Mike stepping down four years earlier, those same trips were wholly different experiences.

Now Mike knew he had to let Michael know a new dynamic was ahead. Michael had grown up, literally, around the business. He'd heard conversations about deals and decisions that many MBA students never find themselves privy to. In many ways, he is wise beyond his years. Just days earlier, Michael had marveled as Mike carried on a Thanksgiving family tradition and personally prepared meals for each of the 30 guests they had invited over for dinner. "When you do that," Michael said in an observation that most pre-teens would not make, "it shows everyone there how much you care for them."

Mike decided the best place to share the news of the impending work change was over dinner…at a Torchy's.

"A few years ago, I had to pawn something dear to me every time payroll rolled around," Mike said as Michael dipped a chip in queso. "I had to beg people to take a chance on me. And now we've grown." Mike nodded at the sea of his own guests. Even though the tables were spread out per six-feet regulations, the restaurant was packed.

"I'm going to get back and be more active with the business and I wanted to tell you, man to man."

Then Michael said the words Mike had always wanted desperately to hear from his own father when he was growing up. "I'm proud of you," young Michael said. "I know how hard you've worked to get us where we are, and I know that you're going to take us to an even higher place. I think you're the best dad."

We...us. The words hung in the air. They were in this together. Mike paused and realized how much he needed them.

The world was right.

Torchy's, Mike, and Michael were all ready for the next chapter.

Afterword

It's early evening in mid-December and Mike is at home in his expansive kitchen in the affluent Lake Austin community. Outside, the sprawling houses etched into the hills are lit up with all manner of imaginative Christmas lighting. Inside, Mike has arrayed 25 boxes filled with holiday cookies he baked himself on the long, black counter that runs the length of the kitchen, the boxes standing in a perfect line, dressed in red and white and a big red bow on top.

"Our neighborhood takes the holiday exchanges very seriously," Mike casually drawls while he dusts the remaining cookies with powdered sugar. And while he chats easily with his guests, he wanders back to his past.

"My mom and I used to bake cookies for the neighborhood," Mike said. "In fact, one of my earliest memories in the kitchen is of me and mom together, baking cookies with Christmas music in the background."

Karen Timmons never tired of boasting about her son, the great chef and restaurateur. More than anyone except Mike himself, or maybe even more than Mike, she knew what demons he had to overcome to get to the point he could feel...what was it? Satisfaction? Simple joy? Belief in himself?

She's there in spirit, of course, sitting in a comfy chair and watching her son move easily around the kitchen and putting the finishing touches on the cookie boxes.

Not many people could do what you have done, she is telling him.

You did alright, son.

No, you did damn good.